BLACKBERRY® PLAYBOOK™

Companion

MATTHEW MILLER

D1310566

WILEY

John Wiley & Sons, Inc.

BlackBerry® PlayBook™ Companion
Published by
John Wiley & Sons, Inc.
10475 Crosspoint Boulevard
Indianapolis, IN 46256
www.wiley.com

Copyright © 2011 by John Wiley & Sons, Inc., Indianapolis, Indiana
Published simultaneously in Canada

ISBN: 978-1-118-02648-9
ISBN: 978-1-118-16819-6 (ebk)
ISBN: 978-1-118-16820-2 (ebk)
ISBN: 978-1-118-16821-9 (ebk)

Manufactured in the United States of America
10 9 8 7 6 5 4 3 2 1

My Savior, Jesus Christ, has blessed me with the technical and writing abilities needed to write this book and everything I have I owe to Him.

—Matthew (palmsolo) Miller

CREDITS

+ ABOUT THE AUTHOR

 **Matthew (palmsolo) Miller** began using mobile devices in 1997 and has been writing about mobile technology since 2001. He is a professional engineer and naval architect in Seattle who served for 12 years in the U.S. Coast Guard after graduating from the United States Coast Guard Academy in 1993.

Matthew began writing daily news posts and conducting reviews for Geek.com in 2001. He co-authored the *Master Visually 2003* book in 2004. In 2006 he launched *The Mobile Gadgeteer* technical blog (`blogs.zdnet.com/mobile-gadgeteer`) on ZDNet and then expanded to his *Smartphone & Cell Phones* blog (`blogs.zdnet.com/cell-phones`) as the smartphone market took off and required a site focused just on mobile phones. Matthew wrote Wiley's *Windows Phone 7 Companion* in December of 2010 and *Facebook Companion* in July of 2011. You can follow Matthew on Twitter at `twitter.com/palmsolo`.

Matthew is also a husband to his beautiful wife of more than 18 years, Dayna, and a father to his three daughters, Danika, Maloree, and Kari. He enjoys playing and coaching sports, camping with the family, and catching all the latest movies.

+ ABOUT THE TECHNICAL EDITOR

Todd Meister has been working in the IT industry for over fifteen years. He's been a Technical Editor on over 75 titles ranging from SQL Server to the .NET Framework. Besides technical editing titles he is the Senior IT Architect at Ball State University in Muncie, Indiana. He lives in central Indiana with his wife, Kimberly, and their four exceptional children.

➕ ACKNOWLEDGMENTS

I would like to thank my wife, Dayna, as she continues to support me for these book projects consuming the majority of my evening hours for a couple of months at a time. Without her encouragement and support, I might not have the motivation to continue with these endeavors that I truly do enjoy. I thank my three wonderful daughters for continuing to give me the hugs I need when I am feeling stressed and for providing some motivation for writing these books, such as college funding.

I want to thank Kevin Michaluk for his willingness to write the Foreword and to help me get answers to my BlackBerry questions. Marissa Conway was also a huge help in securing some accessories to try out and providing an evaluation BlackBerry smartphone to use while writing the book. I thank all my readers at ZDNet who visit my blogs on a regular basis and continue to make daily writing about mobile phones an enjoyable second career. I want to thank Carol Long from Wiley for continuing to be a champion for me and my writing at Wiley. I look forward to continuing to work with her and author more books in the technology field. My project editor at Wiley, Victoria Swider, was amazing to work with, and now that we have done a couple book projects together, I think we have a winning team ready to cover more topics in the near future. Todd Meister did another excellent job in serving as my technical editor, and I appreciate all the editing services provided by San Dee Phillips. A strong editorial team makes a difference in how a book turns out, and I think you will agree this Wiley team did a fantastic job.

+ CONTENTS

Foreword   xi

Introduction   xiii

Chapter 1   **What Is a BlackBerry PlayBook?**   **1**

Walk around the Hardware   2

Walk around the OS   10

Pricing, Availability, and Models   13

Comparison with Other Tablets   13

Related Questions   17

Chapter 2   **How Do I Set Up and Customize My PlayBook?**   **19**

Initial Startup   20

Connect to a Wi-Fi Network   21

Set the Date and Time   26

Create a BlackBerry ID   27

Update Your Software   29

Set Up a BlackBerry Bridge   29

Tablet Basics Tutorials   32

Customize the Home Screen   34

Related Questions   38

Chapter 3   **How Do I Navigate My PlayBook?**   **39**

Utilizing Different Touch Methods   40

Navigating the Home Screen   45

Accessing and Reading Notifications   46

Understanding and Accessing the Status Bar   48

Breaking Down the Menu   50

Switching Between Apps   52

Using the Keyboard   54

Related Questions   57

Chapter 4   **How Do I Surf the Web on My PlayBook?**   **59**

Browsing the Web   60

Changing Browser Options   67

Creating and Managing Bookmarks   73

Managing Downloads   75

Related Questions   76

Chapter 5   **How Do I Bridge the PlayBook with My BlackBerry Smartphone?**   **77**

Set Up the Bridge via Bluetooth   78

Accessing and Using Bridge Files   80

Browsing the Web through the Bridge Browser   82

Using BlackBerry Messenger (BBM) through the Bridge   84

Related Questions   88

Chapter 6   **How Can I Read and Use Email on My PlayBook?**   **89**

Using Email through the Bridge   90

Using Email through the Browser   97

Related Questions   100

Chapter 7   **How Can I Hone My Organizational Skills Using My PlayBook?**   **101**

View Your Calendar   102

Create a New Appointment   107

Manage Contacts   109

Create and View Tasks   112

Create and View Memos   115

Record Voice Notes   116

Related Questions   120

Chapter 8   **How Can I Create, Edit, and View Office Files on My PlayBook?**   **121**

Using Word To Go   122

Using Sheet To Go   131

Using Slideshow To Go   139

Viewing PDF Files   142

Related Questions   144

Chapter 9   How Do I Enjoy Music and Video on My PlayBook?   145

Enjoying Music Loaded onto Your PlayBook   146
Browsing and Purchasing Music through the 7digital Music Store   154
Listening to Music through the Slacker Radio Service   156
Listening to Podcasts   160
Watching Videos   164
BlackBerry PlayBook Video Chat   171
Related Questions   176

**Chapter 10   How Can I View, Share, and Capture Pictures on
My PlayBook?   177**

Transferring Photos on and off Your PlayBook   178
Capturing a Photo   188
Viewing Your Pictures   191
Sharing Your Pictures   194
Related Questions   195

Chapter 11   What Apps Do I Have and How Can I Get More?   197

Using Your Preloaded Apps   198
Finding, Downloading, and Installing Apps via BlackBerry
  App World   216
Related Questions   222

Chapter 12   How Can I Read eBooks on My PlayBook?   223

Using the Kobo eReading Application   224
Using Adobe Reader   236
Related Questions   238

Chapter 13   How Do I Keep My PlayBook Secure?   239

Managing Application Permissions   240
Using Certificates   244
Switching into Development Mode   246
Set, Enable, and Change Your Password   249
Perform a Security Wipe   252
Manage Your VPN Profiles   253
Related Questions   256

Chapter 14 **How Do I Manage Settings on My PlayBook?** **257**

Viewing the About Page 258

Managing Bluetooth Connections 259

Setting Up Internet Tethering 263

Controlling Screen Time-Out and Brightness 267

Setting the HDMI Preferences 268

Managing Your PlayBook Sounds 270

Selecting the General Background Application Settings 271

Managing Your Storage and Sharing Preferences 273

Related Questions 274

Chapter 15 **How Do I Manage My PlayBook with BlackBerry Desktop Software?** **275**

Installing BlackBerry Desktop 276

Desktop Options 279

Device Options 280

Manage Media Sync 283

Back Up Options 284

Switch and Forget Devices 286

Related Questions 286

Chapter 16 **How Do I Troubleshoot My PlayBook?** **287**

General Techniques for Troubleshooting 288

BlackBerry Bridge Issues 292

Browser Issues 293

Wi-Fi Connection Issues 294

Bluetooth Device Connection Issues 294

HDMI Issues 295

Related Questions 295

Index 297

╋ FOREWORD

In the five years I have been working in the mobile space, I've known Matt Miller to be a lot of things: extremely knowledgeable, enthusiastic, forward thinking (I still find it impressive that Matt aka @palmsolo was one of the first 2,500 people on Twitter), a little tech geeky (hence the Twitter early adopter thing) and more.

In that same time frame, one thing I've never known Matt to be was a huge fan of BlackBerry Smartphones. Don't get me wrong; I think Matt has always understood and respected the strengths of the BlackBerry platform and its successes in both enterprise and the consumer marketplace, but aside from liking the great keyboards, I just don't think BlackBerry Smartphones to date have ever been quite cutting edge enough for a guy like Matt who loves technology at its best and brightest. With a phone operating system that's beginning to show its age and hardware specs that have historically lagged the competition, I can't totally hold it against him. But as a long-time BlackBerry fan and founder of CrackBerry.com, the largest BlackBerry website and community on the planet, it's always been one of my goals to turn Matt into a full-fledged BlackBerry addict.

Consider my surprise and delight then, when at 2 p.m. on May 2, 2011, my BlackBerry PlayBook rang with an incoming video chat from Matt Miller, who after letting me know I was the first person he called, declared he absolutely loved his new PlayBook. Finally, a BlackBerry device cutting edge enough to woo Matt! And we are not the only ones worked up about the PlayBook. Our CrackBerry community of more than 3 million members is bursting with excitement for the first tablet from Research In Motion (RIM), the Canadian manufacturer of BlackBerry. You see, the PlayBook isn't like any other BlackBerry before it. The operating system is completely new, built with the demands of today's mobile user and the future in mind. This contrasts the first RIM devices and BlackBerry Smartphones that hit the market more than ten years ago, which featured an operating system designed to be efficient at transferring text data over spotty networks on low-performance hardware. RIM has worked hard over the years and been successful at adapting that operating system to keep up with technological improvements, but you can only renovate so many times before it's time to reboot and build something new from scratch for the future.

It's amazing to think now that Apple's iOS is actually the oldest of the new mobile operating systems on the market. Android, HP/Palm WebOS, and Windows Phone are all newer, and the BlackBerry Tablet OS is the newest. Reinventing themselves has its benefits. With a much clearer vision of where mobile is going than when it released its first RIM two-way pagers, the moment you pick up the BlackBerry PlayBook, you'll appreciate its power and advanced user interface. The ability to power on the display by swiping, use bezel gestures to multitask between apps, and browse full websites thanks to Flash support makes using devices lacking these features feel old school in comparison. (Yes, I'm looking at you iPad.)

Of course, an all-new operating system isn't without its challenges. Though the new BlackBerry Tablet OS has an extremely powerful platform, its *newness* means that it will take time for the device to fill out with apps and OS features. The great news here is that the PlayBook is super easy to update—there's no need to plug it into a computer—and thanks to a myriad of options for developers to choose, the apps should pile up quickly.

Although the BlackBerry PlayBook delivers a relatively intuitive user experience thanks to its touch screen design interface, the PlayBook is full of little gems and advanced features that new users could easily miss. This book will get you up to speed quickly and unlock the full potential of your BlackBerry tablet. And I can't think of a better person to deliver the message than Matt Miller, who's starting to show the signs of a full-fledged BlackBerry addict!

KEVIN MICHALUK
Founder, CrackBerry.com

✛ INTRODUCTION

Research in Motion (RIM) has long ruled the world of QWERTY keyboard smartphones and is now making major efforts to enhance the enterprise experience and appeal to the consumer looking for a large-screen mobile device. The BlackBerry PlayBook is the first device to run the new BlackBerry Tablet OS, based on QNX, and offers a glimpse into what you can expect in 2012 and beyond on BlackBerry smartphones.

You may think the PlayBook is just another BlackBerry, but you can throw those preconceived notions out the window. The PlayBook excels as a mobile web browsing device with a near desktop quality browser and modern finger gesture support. Media is excellent on the PlayBook with an integrated music store, high-resolution rear and front facing cameras that capture videos in high definition, and support for playing videos on the large 7-inch high resolution display.

If you are a BlackBerry user who is used to many hardware buttons and physical keys on your device, you may be shocked to not find a single button on the front of the PlayBook. Navigation, selection, and manipulation of on-screen elements are fully controlled by touch, including gestures made from outside the viewable display onto the display area. There is a Setup Wizard that offers basic training on using the PlayBook when you first turn it on, and I highly recommend you complete it, because you may not know how to control the PlayBook using old habits.

Applications have been rolling out for the PlayBook on a regular basis, and as RIM releases the various software development kits, the number and quality of mobile applications and services is sure to greatly increase.

The PlayBook is a completely new device running a new operating system. I learned more than I ever thought I would while writing this book and hope you are as excited as I am about the potential of this new tablet and mobile operating system from RIM.

CHAPTER ONE

WHAT IS A BLACKBERRY PLAYBOOK?

In this chapter:

+ Walk around the Hardware
+ Walk around the OS
+ Pricing, Availability, and Models
+ Comparison with Other Tablets

C anadian-based Research In Motion (RIM) rolled out the first BlackBerry device in 1999, and since that time it has focused on providing powerful messaging devices that concentrate on enterprise security. RIM has many compelling smartphones available today, with the majority sporting a physical QWERTY keyboard. To help extend the reach of the BlackBerry from the conference room to your living room, RIM released the BlackBerry PlayBook tablet device April 19, 2011. The PlayBook is quite a departure from the QWERTY smartphones they are known for, but as you read in this book, you'll discover the PlayBook retains the essence of BlackBerry while offering compelling consumer functionality. The PlayBook is a fantastic piece of hardware that offers unique experiences when compared to other tablets such as the Apple iPad, Motorola Xoom, and Samsung Galaxy Tab.

Walk around the Hardware

The two most common sizes of tablets today come with displays that are either 7 inches or 10 inches. To make the PlayBook a device that people can carry in their purses, jacket pockets, and with them all the time, RIM went with the smaller 7-inch form factor (see Figure 1-1). As a consumer who has used both sized devices for more than a year, the 7-inch form factor definitely makes the device one that is more likely to be used outside of the home or office.

FIGURE 1-1 RIM BlackBerry PlayBook

Before exploring the device and understanding all the hardware parts, take a look at a list of the specifications:

- 7-inch LCD capacitive touch screen display, with 1024x600 pixels resolution (WSVGA)
- QNX-based BlackBerry Tablet OS
- 1 GHz dual-core processor
- 1GB RAM
- Integrated storage options of 16GB, 32GB, and 64GB
- Dual HD cameras capable of 1080p recording:
  - 5 megapixel rear-facing camera
  - 3 megapixel forward-facing camera
- Stereo speakers
- Micro HDMI video output port
- 802.11 a/b/g/n Wi-Fi radio
- Bluetooth 2.1 + EDR radio
- Integrated GPS receiver
- 5300 mAh battery
- Micro USB port for desktop connection and charging
- Accelerometer
- 6-axis motion sensing gyroscope
- Digital compass (magnetometer)
- Dimensions:
  - Width: 7.6 inches (194 mm)
  - Height: 5.1 inches (130 mm)
  - Depth: 0.4 inches (10 mm)
  - Weight: 15 ounces/0.9lb (425 grams)

When you hold the PlayBook in your hands, you will be amazed that RIM crammed all these great parts into such a sleek and slim form factor.

FRONT OF THE PLAYBOOK

The front of the PlayBook is dominated by the 7-inch resolution display with a black frame measuring approximately 18 mm around all four sides of the viewable area of the display. In addition to the display, you can find speakers, an LED/light sensor, and a forward-facing camera.

WHERE ARE THE BUTTONS? There is not a single hardware or even capacitive touch button on the front of the PlayBook. Navigation is controlled by the touch screen and the surrounding frame that is gesture-sensitive, as detailed in Chapter 3 (How Do I Navigate My PlayBook?).

- **Display**: The display supports up to four-finger multitouch gestures, so you can manipulate objects in unique ways. The capacitive touch screen panel is the type used on modern touch display smartphones, so the bezel responds to your finger rather than a stylus pen. Your finger acts as an electrical conductor and results in a distortion of the screen's electrostatic field, thus changing the capacitance and enabling you to navigate the display. The display supports up to 16 million colors. You can rotate the PlayBook in all four orientations, and the display reorients itself to match your movements, unless you select to lock it. Therefore you can enjoy both widescreen video content and also read in portrait orientation, which closely matches that of a paperback book.

- **Stereo speakers**: Centered on either side of the display are high quality stereo speakers that enable you to turn your PlayBook into a portable media device without even needing to plug in headphones or external speakers (see Figure 1-2).

- **LED indicator/light sensor**: Above the display you can find a small opening in the black frame for the combination notification LED and light sensor (see Figure 1-3). This LED glows red for 3–5 seconds when you power up the PlayBook. It also serves as the light sensor, so in darker environments the screen automatically dims, whereas in well-lit areas the sensor causes the display to brighten.

✦ **Forward facing camera**: To the right of the notification LED, you can find the forward-facing 3 megapixel camera, as shown in Figure 1-3, capable of capturing high-definition video and images. This camera is primarily intended for video conferencing.

FIGURE 1-2 Left stereo speaker grill

FIGURE 1-3 Notification LED and front-facing camera

TOP OF THE PLAYBOOK

Six openings and buttons are located along the top of the PlayBook, which are the following:

+ **Dual microphones**: About 3/4 of an inch in from each side of the top of the PlayBook you can find small holes that serve as openings for microphones, as shown in Figure 1-4. These microphones can record sound in videos, enable you to use the voice recorder application to make voice notes, capture your voice during video chat, and more.

+ **3.5 mm headset jack**: A standard headset jack is on the right side of the top near the edge of the PlayBook (refer to Figure 1-4).

+ **Power button**: Use the small button with red coloring in the center to power on or off your device by pressing and holding, as shown in Figure 1-5. You can also tap it to turn off the display.

- -

SKIP THE POWER BUTTON FOR DISPLAY CONTROL After the launch of the PlayBook, reviewers slammed the device for the nearly flush Power button that was hard to press for display control. You need to press the Power button only once to turn it on; then you can simply use the display timer settings to control when it goes off. Then, simply swipe from the outside of the bezel on any of the four sides into the center to turn the display back on. Because this method saves just as much battery as turning the device off completely, a user rarely turns off her PlayBook so the small Power button is rarely a concern or issue.

- -

+ **Media control buttons**: Centered at the top, just to the right of the Power button, are the Volume Down, Play/Pause, and Volume Up buttons (refer to Figure 1-5). The Play/Pause button works with the default music player, video player, and even third-party applications that use the application programming interface (API). For example, you can control your music with the Play/Pause button in the Slacker Radio and Podcasts applications. To control the volume, press the Volume Up or Down button repeatedly. The volume level appears in a pop-up in the center of the display, and there are 15 volume levels. If you hold down either one of the volume controls, it simply turns off the on-screen volume level display.

FIGURE 1-4 Headset jack and microphone opening

FIGURE 1-5 Power and media control buttons

QUICK MUTE TOGGLE You can toggle the mute function on and off by simply pressing and holding the Play/Pause button. A red Speaker icon with a line through it indicates that mute is enabled and another press/ hold turns on the speakers at the level you had set previously.

CAPTURE SCREENSHOTS WITH THE VOLUME BUTTONS A favorite trick for those who write books, reviews, or provide feedback to developers is to capture a photograph of your computer screen. To capture what you see on your PlayBook display, simply press the Volume Up and Volume Down buttons simultaneously. Screenshots are captured as .JPG images with 1024 x 600 pixels resolution and are placed in the camera roll just like when you capture still photos with one of the PlayBook cameras.

BOTTOM OF THE PLAYBOOK

The bottom has some labeling information on either side with three important ports. These are described in the following list:

✦ **Labeling**: On the left side of the bottom is where you can find the integrated storage stamp designating which of the three available models (16GB, 32GB, and 64GB) you have. Labeling on the right side includes the manufacturer's data.

✦ **HDMI port**: A micro HDMI port enables you to connect to your PlayBook with a compatible cable to an HD TV or monitor and output your display to the big screen (see Figure 1-6).

✦ **Micro USB port**: The micro USB port is used for both charging and data transfer and is standard in most modern smartphones, including your BlackBerry smartphone (refer to Figure 1-6).

✦ **Charging contacts**: There is an opening with three small gold contacts that you can use with compatible accessories to charge up your PlayBook (refer to Figure 1-6). The BlackBerry Rapid Charging Pad and Rapid Travel Charger both connect to these charging contacts to power up your PlayBook.

FIGURE 1-6 HDMI, micro USB, and charging ports

BACK OF THE PLAYBOOK

The back of your PlayBook is entirely coated in black soft-touch material, eliminating messy fingerprints like you see on glossy black plastic finishes (see Figure 1-7).

FIGURE 1-7 Back of the PlayBook

The soft-touch coating also helps you hold onto the PlayBook better. Only two things are on the back of the PlayBook:

➕ **BlackBerry logo**: The BlackBerry logo is highlighted in shiny silver material and placed directly in the middle of the back.

➕ **Rear facing camera**: The 5-megapixel rear-facing camera is centered near the top of the back of your PlayBook, as shown in Figure 1-8. As you can see, there is no flash with this camera. This camera is primarily used to capture photos and videos while using the large display as your viewfinder.

FIGURE 1-8 Rear-facing 5-megapixel camera

RETAIL BOX CONTENTS

The RIM BlackBerry PlayBook comes in an attractive retail package, and includes the following inside the box:

- Neoprene sleeve/case with BlackBerry branding
- A/C charger with micro USB male end
- USB to micro USB cable
- Screen cleaning cloth
- Product warranty and safety brochures

It is quite rare to find any type of case in the box with today's mobile devices, so it is a nice touch to have the neoprene sleeve case, as shown in Figure 1-9, that provides some basic protection for the PlayBook. HDMI to micro HDMI cables do not come standard with the device so you need to purchase one from your local electronics retailer or online retailer to output your PlayBook's display to a big screen via the micro HDMI port.

FIGURE 1-9 Included neoprene slip case

Walk around the OS

In September 2010, RIM co-CEO Mike Lazaridis said, "RIM set out to engineer the best professional-grade tablet in the industry with cutting-edge hardware features and one of the world's most robust and flexible operating systems.

The BlackBerry PlayBook solidly hits the mark with industry-leading power, true multitasking, uncompromised web browsing, and high performance multimedia." RIM created their BlackBerry Tablet OS using a base of QNX and focused on supporting developers with a number of design platforms.

INTRODUCTION TO QNX NEUTRINO REALTIME OPERATING SYSTEM (RTOS)

The QNX Neutrino microkernel architecture that the BlackBerry Tablet OS is built upon has been in use for many years. Neutrino has been used in important system applications such as airplanes, trains, automobiles, medical equipment, the International Space Station, and the large core routers that run the Internet. Thus, the foundation for the BlackBerry Tablet OS is well proven and trusted.

The microkernel architecture, as opposed to the monolithic kernel architecture, enables functions, drivers, and file systems to operate outside of the kernel space, in user space, and thus the entire system does not need to shut down if a part of the OS crashes. The QNX Neutrino-based platform focuses on stability and performance for essential functions, rather than customization or flashy visual effects. The PlayBook has wonderful graphics, fluid performance in games, and amazing support for applications, but the focus is on an experience that performs well.

Neutrino also provides RIM with the capability to support a large number of diverse application development environments, as discussed in the following section.

DEVELOPMENT ENVIRONMENTS SUPPORTED ON THE PLAYBOOK

The BlackBerry Tablet OS is Portable Operating System Interface (POSIX)-compliant, which means a level of code portability exists between systems to support software interoperability so applications created now for the PlayBook will run on future BlackBerry smartphones that may be running a different variation of the OS. Playbook supports a number of SDKs and development environments, including the following:

+ **BlackBerry Tablet OS Native Development Kit (NDK)**: Enables C/C++ application development with the highest level of performance and support for OpenGL graphics functions

- **BlackBerry WebWorks SDK**: Supports the HTML5 web development standard
- **BlackBerry Tablet SDK for Adobe Air**: Supports development through Adobe Air
- **BlackBerry Java SDK and app player**: Enables consumers to run apps in a secure "sandboxed" area
- **Android app player**: Supports Android 2.3 apps

In addition to these environments, the web browser on the PlayBook is built to run WebKit and Adobe Flash, so web apps can also be used on the PlayBook. Applications are submitted to RIM and then appear in the BlackBerry App World application store.

BlackBerry Tablet OS Native Development Kit (NDK)

The NDK is the optimal environment to use when developing for the PlayBook with applications that can take advantage of the advanced 2D and 3D support on the device and hardware-accelerated OpenGL ES 2.0. As stated in the RIM press release at launch, other features of the BlackBerry Tablet OS NDK enable developers to:

- Take advantage of the QNX POSIX library support and C/C++ compliance for quick-and-easy application porting and for creating native extensions for both BlackBerry and Android applications.
- Easily integrate device events such as gesture swipes and touch screen inputs.
- Integrate the BlackBerry Tablet OS environment into existing code management and build systems using industry standard Eclipse CDT (C/C++ Development Tools).
- Leverage work done in standard C/C++ to make it easier to bring applications to the BlackBerry Tablet OS.
- Find and fix bugs quickly with proven debug and analysis tools.
- Produce games using game development tools from Unity Technologies and Ideaworks Labs.

Pricing, Availability, and Models

As of the PlayBook launch, there are three BlackBerry Playbook models available to choose from, and all three of these models support Wi-Fi-only, with no integrated cellular data radio. The three options include:

+ 16GB for $499
+ 32GB for $599
+ 64GB for $699

In the United States, sales launched at Best Buy, Office Depot, OfficeMax, RadioShack, Staples, and through the RIM online store. RIM announced that models with integrated cellular data would be coming in the future that include support for WiMAX, HSPA+, and LTE network technologies. These models will be available from carriers, and it is likely that subsidized price offerings will be available, so you can purchase a PlayBook for less money up front (generally a $100 to $200 savings for tablets) with a 1-year or 2-year service contract and minimum monthly data plan. The following models will become available throughout the course of 2011:

+ BlackBerry PlayBook with Wi-Fi 802.1 a/b/g/n (available now)
+ BlackBerry 4G PlayBook with Wi-Fi 802.11 a/b/g/n + WiMax (Sprint network)
+ BlackBerry 4G PlayBook with Wi-Fi 802.11 a/b/g/n + LTE (Verizon and maybe AT&T)
+ BlackBerry 4G PlayBook with Wi-Fi 802.11 a/b/g/n + HSPA+ (T-Mobile, AT&T, and non-U.S. networks)

Comparison with Other Tablets

Although tablet devices existed before 2010, Apple launched its iPad line in April 2010 and has sold millions. Thus, every tablet launched since then is first compared to the Apple iPad, and you can take a look at how the PlayBook stacks up to it in the following section. Since then, Google has developed compelling tablet offerings running the Android operating system. The Motorola Xoom and Samsung Galaxy Tab are the best-selling Android tablets that also compare well with the PlayBook. Tablets running HP's webOS and many more Android tablets will also be launched in 2011.

APPLE IPAD

Apple launched the iPad 2 in March 2011 with 18 different models available, including the following:

- White or black
- 16GB, 32GB, or 64GB internal memory capacity
- Wi-Fi only
- AT&T or Verizon 3G cellular data radio plus Wi-Fi

As detailed in the previous section, the RIM BlackBerry PlayBook launched with Wi-Fi-only models in 16GB, 32GB, and 64GB capacities and is priced exactly the same as the iPad 2 devices with the same memory capacities.

Now take a look at some key differences in the specifications and features between the PlayBook and the Apple iPad:

TABLE 1-1: iPad 2 versus PlayBook

SPECIFICATION	APPLE IPAD 2	BLACKBERRY PLAYBOOK
Display size and resolution	9.7" at 1024×768	7" at 1024×600
Processor	Apple A5 dual-core 1GHz	ARM Cortex A9 dual-core 1GHZ
Cameras	<1 megapixel with 720p video	5 megapixel rear and 3 megapixel still capacity with 1080p video
Adobe Flash	No	Yes
Third-party apps	More than 75,000	More than 2,500

MOTOROLA XOOM

The Motorola Xoom was the first Android 3.0 device, also known as Honeycomb. Android 3.0 was designed for the tablet form factor, and the

Xoom launched in the United States from Verizon Wireless in February 2011. A Wi-Fi-only version started selling from various retailers in the United States and Canada in March 2011.

The Xoom comes with 32GB of integrated memory and a microSD card slot for expanded storage. As of May 2011, the microSD card slot is not yet usable because a firmware update is required to enable it. The Verizon Xoom launched with support for 3G data at a price of $599.99 with a 2-year Verizon contract and minimum monthly data price. You could buy it without a contract for $799.99 as well. The Wi-Fi-only model sells for $599 and no contract is required.

$599 IS A STANDARD PRICE The 32GB models of the Wi-Fi-only Apple iPad, Motorola Xoom, and BlackBerry PlayBook are all priced at $599, so price is taken out of the equation when evaluating which tablet device meets your needs.

Now take a look at some key differences in the specifications and features between the RIM BlackBerry PlayBook and the Motorola Xoom:

TABLE 1-2: Motorola Xoom versus PlayBook

SPECIFICATION	MOTOROLA XOOM	BLACKBERRY PLAYBOOK
Display size and resolution	10.1" at 1280x800	7" at 1024x600
Processor	NVIDIA Tegra 2 dual-core 1GHz	ARM Cortex A9 dual-core 1GHZ
Cameras	5 megapixel rear and 2 megapixel still capacity with 720p video	5 megapixel rear and 3 megapixel still capacity with 1080p video
Adobe Flash	Yes	Yes
Third-party apps	More than 60	More than 2,500

SAMSUNG GALAXY TAB

The Samsung Galaxy Tab is available as a 7-inch form factor tablet with new, larger 8.9-inch and 10.1-inch models launching later in 2011. The Galaxy Tab was the first major Android tablet to challenge the iPad in the tablet market and sold quite well with more than 2 million reportedly sold between November 2010 and February 2011.

The Samsung Galaxy Tab is available now from various mobile carriers around the world and also as a Wi-Fi-only model. If you are looking for a tablet that is smaller than the iPad, larger than Android tablets or HP webOS tablets, then the Samsung Galaxy Tab is the closest competitor to the BlackBerry PlayBook. It can be purchased for a subsidized price ranging from $199.99 to $249.99, with the requirement of a 2-year data contract. The unsubsidized price is $549.99. A Wi-Fi only model is available for $349.99.

Now take a look at some key differences in the specifications and features between the RIM BlackBerry PlayBook and the Samsung Galaxy Tab:

TABLE 1-3: Galaxy Tab versus PlayBook

SPECIFICATION	SAMSUNG GALAXY TAB	BLACKBERRY PLAYBOOK
Display size and resolution	7" at 1024×600	7" at 1024×600
Processor	ARM Cortex A8 1GHZ	ARM Cortex A9 dual-core 1GHZ
Cameras	3 megapixel rear and 1.3 megapixel still capacity with 720p video	5 megapixel rear and 3 megapixel still capacity with 1080p video
Adobe Flash	Yes	Yes
Third-party apps	More than 100,000, not all tablet-optimized	More than 2,500

A major difference between the available tablets is the number of applications available for the different platforms. The quantity isn't as important as the quality, but more choices inevitably result in a better selection and higher quality to choose from. RIM is still in its infancy with the BlackBerry App World on the PlayBook because only limited developer tools were released by May 2011. As developers get the opportunity to use the native development kit (NDK), bring BlackBerry smartphone apps to the PlayBook, and update Android apps to work with the Android Player, you will have many more apps to choose from on the PlayBook. RIM also focused on bringing a desktop-class browser to the PlayBook so that the need for apps in many cases can be eliminated by accessing tools via the web browser.

Related Questions

- How can I enjoy music through the stereo speakers? **PAGE 146**
- The PlayBook cameras look good, but how can I use them to capture photos and videos? **PAGE 188**
- Where can I find out more about third party applications available for the PlayBook? **PAGE 216**

CHAPTER TWO

HOW DO I SET UP AND CUSTOMIZE MY PLAYBOOK?

In this chapter:

+ Initial Startup

+ Connect to a Wi-Fi Network

+ Set the Date and Time

+ Create a BlackBerry ID

+ Update Your Software

+ Set Up a BlackBerry Bridge

+ Tablet Basics Tutorials

+ Customize the Home Screen

I f you already own a BlackBerry PlayBook, then you have likely completed the startup and customization steps detailed in this chapter. However, this chapter covers each of the startup screens in detail, so you may find the need to go back and change some settings to optimize your tablet. For those interested in the PlayBook, this chapter describes the out-of-box experience after powering on the PlayBook for the first time.

Initial Startup

To make sure that you achieve an optimal battery experience, it is recommended that you plug in your BlackBerry PlayBook prior to the first startup. You can fully charge it prior to using or walk through the set-up while it is plugged in. To access your PlayBook for the first time, follow these two steps:

1. Press the Power button and the display turns on to the Welcome screen, as shown in Figure 2-1.

2. You'll need to be connected to a Wi-Fi network to begin setup, so make sure you are in range of an accessible one prior to proceeding.

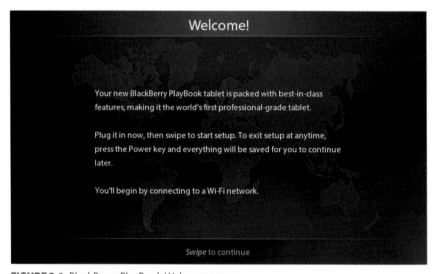

FIGURE 2-1 BlackBerry PlayBook Welcome screen

3. At the bottom of the Welcome screen, swipe your finger from right to left to continue the startup process. The scrolling light and white circle passing across the bottom indicate the direction for you to swipe.

YOU CAN COME BACK LATER If you started the setup and do not have access to a Wi-Fi network or decide you do not want to complete the setup routine at this time, you can simply press the Power button, and everything will be saved in the state you left it so that you can continue at a later time.

Connect to a Wi-Fi Network

After swiping on the Welcome screen, you see the Connect to Wi-Fi display appear, as shown in Figure 2-2. Available networks appear in a list starting in the upper-left corner of your display. In the bottom-left corner, you can find options to manually connect to a network, setup a Wi-Fi-protected connection, and access diagnostic information (indicated with the Gear icon).

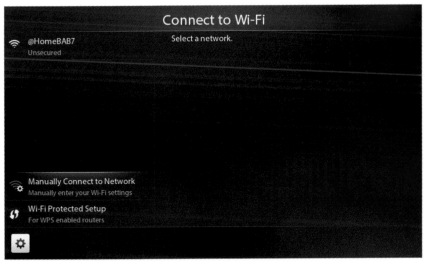

FIGURE 2-2 Connect to Wi-Fi screen.

If you tap on the Gear icon in the bottom-left corner, a diagnostic screen appears, as shown in Figure 2-3, with the following information for your PlayBook. This information is primarily used by customer service representatives to assist you if you experience an issue with your PlayBook.

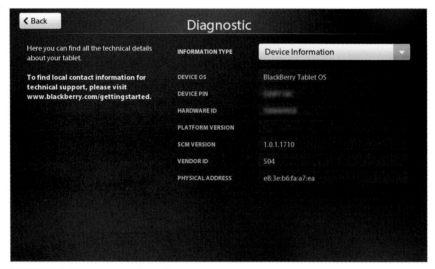

FIGURE 2-3 Diagnostics information

+ **Information type**: Choose from a drop-down list of the following options:
  + Device Information
  + Wi-Fi Information
  + Internet Connection
  + Logs
  + Ping
+ **Device OS:** This option shows the BlackBerry Tablet OS that is installed on your PlayBook.
+ **Device PIN:** This is an eight digit string of numbers and letters that is used to identify your specific device.
+ **Hardware ID:** This number identifies your hardware.
+ **Platform Version:** This option displays the version of the software platform loaded on your PlayBook

- **SCM Version:** This field is also used to state the software version loaded on your PlayBook and in the future may not appear in the diagnostic data since it is used interchangeably with the platform version field.

- **Vendor ID:** This is an ID number for RIM.

- **Physical address:** This is the MAC address for your PlayBook.

CONNECTING TO A LISTED NETWORK

If you want to connect to one of the networks in the upper-left list, simply tap on the network name, and a couple of options appear in the center of the display, depending on the network security settings and whether you have the Simple/Advanced toggle selected. For an unsecured network with the Advanced toggle active, you can find check boxes for the following two options:

- **Automatically Obtain IP Address and DNS**: Here your PlayBook makes the connection automatically with the wireless network you select.

- **Use HTTP Proxy**: Some wireless networks require that you proxy into them, and by selecting this option you will be presented with proxy settings that need to be entered before making the connection.

If the network you want to connect with is a secured network, you see the same preceding options with a password entry field, as shown in Figure 2-4:

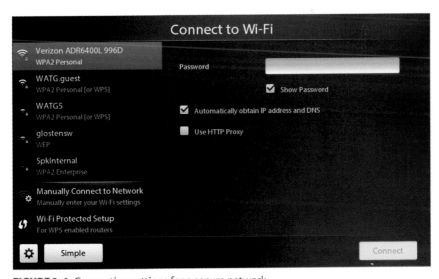

FIGURE 2-4 Connection settings for a secure network

After making the selections required for your network type, tap on the large Connect button in the lower-right part of your display to connect to Wi-Fi.

MANUALLY CONNECT TO A NETWORK

You may need to connect to a network that has a hidden SSID and other special network settings that don't enable you to connect automatically. If this applies to your situation, tap the option to Manually Connect to a Network, and the following options appear on the display:

- **SSID name entry field**: Enter the service set identifier (SSID) for your network. This is typically the name of the network.

- **Hidden SSID check box**: Open networks generally have a public broadcast SSID, but if you connect to a network that does not broadcast the SSID then you need to check the box so you can manually enter the SSID.

- **Security type drop-down**: The following options appear for each selected security type:

  - **Open**: No additional settings

  - **WEP**: Text entry box to enter password and check box to toggle Show Password on and off

  - **WPA and WPA2 Personal**: Text entry box to enter password and check box to toggle Show Password on and off

  - **WPA and WPA2 Enterprise**: Provide the highest level of security with many options for you to configure. You will likely need to contact your IT department to discuss these settings. Depending on the type of security sub type you choose (PEAP, TTLS, FAST, TLS) you will see the following:

    - **Username**

    - **Password**

    - **CA Certificate**: A long list of installed certificates to choose from. Certificate Authority (CA) is an entity that issues digital certificates. By default RIM includes several to choose from.

    - **Client Certificate**: Your company may also have specific certificates for verifying your connection.

- **VPN Profiles**: Your company may use Virtual Private Network (VPN) to connect so you can select a profile and login if the network supports it.

- **Band type (Dual band, 2.4 GHz, or 5 GHz)**: Your router may support just one of these two frequencies, but in most cases choose dual band since it enables your PlayBook to automatically figure out which band is being used by the router.

- **Automatically obtain IP address**: If you uncheck this box, then you need to enter the IP address, subnet mask, and primary DNS data manually. Most of the time, leaving this box checked is satisfactory.

- **Enable IPv6**: Internet Protocol version 6 (IPv6) is replacing the current generation protocol with support for more bandwidth. This is checked by default.

- **Use HTTP Proxy check box**: Some networks have an intermediate computer that you pass through to gain internet access. If you connect through this proxy, check the box and then enter the proxy server, proxy port, username, and password.

- **Allow interaccess point handover**: If you try to connect to a network for a large company or organization that has multiple routers on a single network, then you may have to enable this functionality to allow your PlayBook to be handed off as you move around the office.

After manually setting up your network connection, tap the Save button and then the Connect button to make the connection with your PlayBook.

WI-FI PROTECTED SETUP (WPS)

Wi-Fi Protected Setup enables you to use buttons or PIN codes instead of entering all the settings detailed earlier to set up a network. You must have a WPS-compatible router to use WPS. To use this option, follow these steps:

1. Select the WPS option on your Wi-Fi Network on your Connect to Wi-Fi display and you can see two buttons appear.

2. Press the first button. As this button indicates, press the WPS button on the router, then tap the Start button on your PlayBook; your connection should be made between your PlayBook and the WPS router.

3. Press the second button and the Start button that appears on the next screen. Enter the 8-digit PIN code that appears into your router for the secure connection to be made.

After completing the setup for a Wi-Fi network connection and making a connection active, swipe from right to left to continue the initial setup process.

Set the Date and Time

The Date and Time section shown in Figure 2-5 gives you the option to have the date and time set automatically. Follow these steps to do so:

1. Slide the toggle switch and the current date and time at the bottom of the display is grayed out. (If you ever turn off automatic time, you can tap on the date and time and set it to match the current time.)

2. Choose how you want your time displayed on the 24-Hour Time toggle (the automatic setting is Off).

3. Manually select your time zone, (even with the time and date set to automatic) because the PlayBook does not automatically determine your location.

4. When you finish choosing your time settings, slide your finger from right to left to continue the setup process.

FIGURE 2-5 Date and Time

Create a BlackBerry ID

A BlackBerry ID is required prior to using your new PlayBook, but one step precedes creating this ID or logging in with it: comply with the BlackBerry ID Agreement. The Agreement is a legal agreement between RIM and you. To comply with this agreement, follow these steps:

1. Select the country you are in and then the applicable agreement appears on the screen, as shown in Figure 2-6.

2. Read the agreement (swipe from top to bottom to scroll further down the page) and tap on the I Agree choice to continue using your PlayBook. If you tap I Do Not Agree, the Setup Wizard stops and you cannot use your PlayBook.

3. After selecting the I Agree option, slide your finger from right to left to continue.

The BlackBerry ID is used as a single sign-in to BlackBerry sites, services, and applications, much like a Gmail login for Android devices or a Live.com login for Windows Phone devices. If you already have a BlackBerry ID, simply enter your ID username and password.

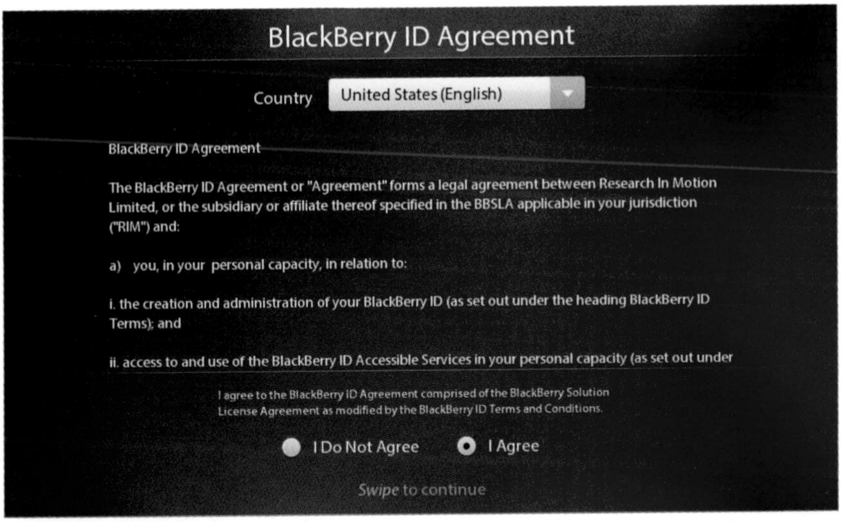

FIGURE 2-6 BlackBerry ID agreement

- -

OOPS, I FORGOT MY BLACKBERRY ID PASSWORD There is a button to tap if you forgot your password; do so and then enter your email address to have a reset email sent to you. After receiving that email on your computer or other device, follow the steps to reset your password.

- -

If you do not have a BlackBerry ID, you can tap the option to create one and then fill out the following on the creation page:

- **Username**: Enter a valid email address.

- **Screen Name**: This is used to identify you without revealing personal info, such as when you post app reviews in BlackBerry App World.

- **Password**: Must be at least eight characters.

- **Confirm Password**: Retype your password.

- **Enter a Question**: Enter a security question (in case you forget your password).

After you log in with an existing account or finish creating a new one, the success page appears, noting that this step of the process is complete (see Figure 2-7). Swipe your finger from right to left to continue the process.

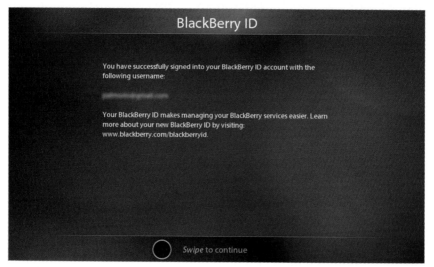

FIGURE 2-7 Successfully signed in

Update Your Software

Your PlayBook automatically checks to see if there is an available software update since your device was boxed up for some time prior to your purchase. Depending on when RIM releases updates, you may not see an available update during the setup process. If your PlayBook finds a software update available during this step it begins downloading the update automatically (see Figure 2-8). It will then auto restart after the update is done and will be taken back to this step in the setup process.

FIGURE 2-8 Updating your software

Set Up a BlackBerry Bridge

This next step requires you to have a BlackBerry smartphone; if you do not have one, you can skip this step entirely. If you purchase a BlackBerry smartphone in the future, you can set up the Bridge later through the PlayBook settings. BlackBerry Bridge enables you to connect to a BlackBerry smartphone via a Bluetooth wireless connection and provides access to your email, text messages, contacts, calendar, memo pad, tasks, and files from the PlayBook. You also gain the ability to access the web browser through your smartphone data connection rather than needing to connect via Wi-Fi to use the web browser.

To access the initial set-up screen, follow these steps:

1. Tap the Set Up BlackBerry Bridge button in the center of the display (see Figure 2-9).

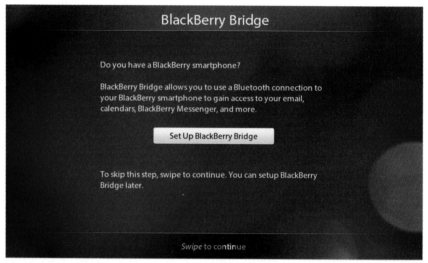

FIGURE 2-9 Getting ready to set up the BlackBerry Bridge

2. Choose a name for your PlayBook tablet; then tap the Next button.

3. To use BlackBerry Bridge you need a software utility installed on your compatible BlackBerry smartphone. Tap on the Install Now button to ensure you install it correctly. Another Bridge setup page appears with a set of numbered instructions. Follow these steps, as shown in Figure 2-10.

4. After installation on your BlackBerry smartphone is complete, tap the Back button in the upper-left corner of your PlayBook to return to the setup pages.

OTHER WAYS TO GET BRIDGE SOFTWARE ON YOUR SMARTPHONE
If the scan feature does not work, you can use your BlackBerry browser to visit `www.bbry.lv/BlackBerryBridge` or enter the search term `BlackBerry Bridge` into your App World search box.

Now that you have the BlackBerry Bridge software installed on your smartphone, you need to pair your smartphone with your PlayBook. The BlackBerry Bridge setup screen changes into pairing mode. Follow the instructions on this screen, as shown in Figure 2-11, to pair the two:

FIGURE 2-10 Scan to get the smartphone software.

FIGURE 2-11 Scan to pair devices.

If you cannot use the scan feature for pairing, you can tap the Manual Pairing button and then follow the Setup Wizard to make the pairing happen. After pairing is complete, a success screen appears, as shown in Figure 2-12, showing you that a BlackBerry Bridge category will appear on your Home screen with icons for all the supported Bridge apps. Again, swipe your finger from right to left to continue the setup process.

FIGURE 2-12 Successfully paired Bridge setup

Tablet Basics Tutorials

You are almost at the end of the out-of-box setup experience, and RIM has a couple of tutorials available for you to view and learn a bit more about your new device. Because the PlayBook user interface is unlike any BlackBerry you have ever used, RIM requires new PlayBook owners to launch both the Home screen and App menu tutorials (see Figure 2-13). If you do not launch both of these, you cannot proceed to the next step and use your device.

The PlayBook tutorials teach you a bit about how to navigate the device, but read on to Chapter 3 (How Do I Navigate My PlayBook?) for more detailed information on that process. The tutorials touch on the following:

+ Using the touch-sensitive frame.

+ Accessing the Home screen via the frame.

+ View menus via the frame.

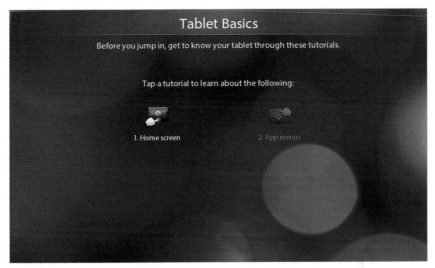

FIGURE 2-13 Two available tutorials

The final page of the setup is a summary of what setup actions you have completed, as shown in Figure 2-14. The sections with a green check mark indicate completion, whereas those without still need to be completed. Note that the Desktop section is not completed in Figure 2-14. Read Chapter 15 (How Do I Manage My PlayBook with BlackBerry Desktop Software?) to discover how to connect your Windows PC to your PlayBook.

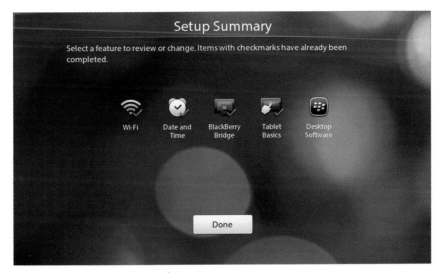

FIGURE 2-14 Setup is now complete.

You can tap on any section to review or edit the settings. Tap the Done button to finish the out-of-box setup procedure, and you will be taken to your PlayBook Home screen.

Customize the Home Screen

Your Blackberry PlayBook allows for a few customizations that make your user experience that much more enjoyable. These include changing your wallpaper and moving or uninstalling apps.

SET WALLPAPER

The wallpaper on your PlayBook is a static image, and by default a RIM colored one is present. To change your wallpaper image, follow these steps:

1. Tap the Pictures application, found under the All and Media tabs on the Home screen.

2. Find a photo on your PlayBook you want to use as your wallpaper, and tap it to open in the viewer. Choose a stock photo or see Chapter 10 (How Can I View, Share, and Capture Pictures on My PlayBook?) to learn how to take one of your own.

3. Slide your finger from the upper frame down toward the center to open the Pictures menus (see Figure 2-15).

4. Tap the Set as Wallpaper icon on the far right to select your photos as the wallpaper image.

OPTIMAL SIZE FOR WALLPAPER IMAGES If you notice your photo automatically cropping in an undesirable manner, make sure your photo is 1024x1024 so that it scales properly in both landscape and portrait orientations. Other resolutions may cause random cropping.

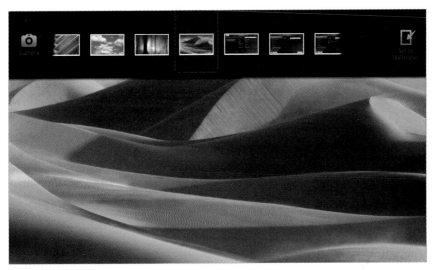

FIGURE 2-15 Setting a photo as wallpaper

MOVE APPS

Your PlayBook comes preloaded with five organizational categories, called tabs. These include:

- All
- Favorites
- Media
- Games
- BlackBerry Bridge

Additionally, several default applications (apps) come preloaded on your PlayBook. These appear on the All tab in a rather random order, and the ones you install manually through the BlackBerry App World appear in the order in which you install them. These categories and locations may or may not be the manner in which you prefer to organize your apps; therefore, to enhance your PlayBook user experience, you have the option to move your apps around within the Home screen tab or categorize them in another tab completely.

To move your apps, simply touch and hold on an icon until it starts pulsing. You can then drag and drop icons within a Home screen tab. If you want to add apps to a different category, drag the icon over one of the aforementioned tab names to copy the shortcut into that tab.

COPIES OF APPS REMAIN IN ALL, TOO   Apps placed in Favorites, Media, Games, or BlackBerry Bridge always appear in All, unless they are uninstalled, so you can always find them.

TAP THE LEFT DOWN ARROW TO STOP THE PULSING   After you place the icon and leave it in its new location, you may see the icons continue to pulse. To get them to stop, tap on the down arrow found in the upper-left side of the display.

UNINSTALL APPS

While you can move and place all of your apps anywhere you like, you are limited on which apps you can permanently uninstall. All apps that you install can be uninstalled. Most all of the included apps are part of the operating system and cannot be removed by you, such as Pictures, Music, Camera and more. These are the only apps pre-loaded on your PlayBook that you can uninstall:

+ Slacker Radio
+ Kobo Books
+ Adobe Reader
+ Included browser shortcuts for Gmail, Hotmail, Yahoo! Mail, and Twitter

Apps that you can uninstall appear with a small trash can symbol below the icon and application name (see Figure 2-16). To uninstall one of these apps, follow these steps:

1. Tap on the trash can symbol below the application icon.
2. A dialog pop-up appears, as shown in Figure 2-17, asking if you want to delete the application and associated data from your PlayBook. You can tap the Cancel button if you do not want to uninstall the selected app.

FIGURE 2-16 Apps with Trash Can icons can be removed.

FIGURE 2-17 Uninstall an App.

Related Questions

✦ How do I use my BlackBerry ID with App World? **PAGE 222**

✦ What can I do with the BlackBerry Bridge? **PAGE 80**

✦ In addition to a secure connection, how else can I keep my PlayBook secure? **PAGE 240**

CHAPTER THREE

HOW DO I NAVIGATE MY PLAYBOOK?

In this chapter:

+ Utilizing Different Touch Methods
+ Navigating the Home Screen
+ Accessing and Reading Notifications
+ Understanding and Accessing the Status Bar
+ Breaking Down the Menu
+ Switching Between Apps
+ Using the Keyboard

hapter 2 (How Do I Set Up and Customize My Playbook?) went through the setup process on your new PlayBook. There you learned some of the basics about the unique touch screen user interface made possible by the BlackBerry Tablet OS. This chapter provides a more in-depth look at all the gestures that include the finger swipe, pinch, drag, tap, and touch and hold that you use to navigate and control your PlayBook. Discover where to find the upper menus, Status bar, touch screen keyboard, notifications, and more on your device—all accessible with just a touch.

Utilizing Different Touch Methods

After you turn on your PlayBook and complete the setup, the Home screen appears with loads of shortcuts to various applications, games, utilities, and web browser bookmarks, as shown in Figure 3-1. No buttons appear around the display, and none of the media buttons on the top enable you to navigate around the display. As pointed out in Chapter 1 (What Is a BlackBerry PlayBook?) the frame around the display is touch-sensitive and integral to manipulating the device.

FIGURE 3-1 Home screen view

The key gestures to navigate the device include the following:

+ Swipe

+ Tap

+ Touch and hold

+ Drag

+ Pinch together and apart

This section covers each of these actions in detail because there are different areas where you perform these actions, and you need to gain proficiency with all these methods.

SWIPE

Swiping is a fluid and natural way to move around your PlayBook. The first action you performed after turning on your PlayBook was a swipe from right to left to get past the Welcome screen. RIM displayed a white marquee light scrolling through the words "Swipe to Continue" from right to left and a large white circle sliding over the top of the words, simulating your finger motion. A *swipe* is a constant movement of your finger from one area of the display to another in a manner where your finger rests on the display at all times. You can swipe up, down, right, left, and even diagonally. The following functions are controlled by swiping on the PlayBook:

+ **Turn on the display**: Swipe your finger up, down, left, or right across at least half of the display (vertically or horizontally) to wake up the display when it is off while the power is on.

+ **Access the Home screen**: From within any application, swipe up from the lower frame into the center of the display to go to the Home screen. This action works in both portrait and landscape orientations.

+ **Toggle the Application View**: When you have open applications minimized, you can show active panels (large thumbnails) of these apps in a "cover flow" format at the top of your screen (see Figure 3-2). If you swipe up from the lower frame of the Home screen, you can toggle this cover flow view on and off.

FIGURE 3-2 Minimized applications in cover flow

+ **Access top menus**: In some applications, swiping down from the top frame opens application-specific menu options.

ACCESS SETTINGS FROM THE HOME SCREEN Although swiping down from the top in applications generally opens up the top menu, if you perform this same action on the Home screen you go directly to the PlayBook settings area.

+ **Access the Status bar**: The Status bar is present on the Home screen, covered later in this chapter, but if you want to access it from within an application, swipe down diagonally from either of the top two corners. If you swipe down again the same way, you can toggle off the Status bar.

+ **Access the keyboard**: Swipe up diagonally from the bottom-left corner to access the keyboard if you are not in a text entry field where the keyboard appears automatically. Like the Status bar diagonal swipe, you can swipe again here to toggle the keyboard off.

✚ **Scroll through objects**: You can swipe right or left to scroll through different Home screen tabs, active apps in cover flow, photos in the photo gallery, pages of an eBook, lists, and more.

✚ **Pan on a page**: If you are on a website, viewing a photo, in a document, or within another page full of information, you can swipe up, down, right, and left to pan through the page.

✚ **Close an app**: On the Home screen you can touch a minimized app thumbnail image and swipe it up off the top to close the application.

TAP

A *tap* is a quick, hard press and release of the finger on the display screen. To select something, activate a button, or expand a drop-down list, you need to tap on an object.

TAP INSTEAD OF SWIPE You often see small gray arrows to the right or left of an area, and you can simply tap these instead of swiping to perform the same action (minimize, maximize, and more).

Taps are used for the following reasons:

✚ **Select an object**: When you find a menu you want to access, a button you want to press, a drop-down list you want to view, or another object that you want to select, simply tap on it once to perform the action or open up more details for the object.

✚ **Launch an application**: To launch an app, tap on the application icon from the Home screen.

✚ **Auto zoom**: If you are already zoomed in on a web page, photo, or other object, you can double-tap on the object to auto-zoom back out to a readable level. For example, on a web page, double-tap you will be taken in to a zoom level so that the selected area fills the width of the display. Double-tapping again zooms you back out to the level you were previously in before your first double-tap.

TOUCH AND HOLD

You can also touch and hold by pressing and leaving your finger on the display screen for a few seconds in preparation of performing another action. Touch and holds are used in conjunction with other gestures, and most typically precede a tap. Touch and holds are used to perform the following functions:

✚ **Move an application icon**: To move an application icon or place one into a different subheading on the Home screen, touch and hold on it; then drag it to where you want it to appear.

✚ **Access advance options**: Touching and holding within applications can present you with a number of different functions. For example, if you touch and hold a hyperlink in the web browser for a couple seconds, you can see options to open a link, open a link in a new tab, copy a link, save a link as, and cancel the command, as shown in Figure 3-3. If you touch and hold on a photo in the browser you see options to open the link, open it in a new tab, copy the link, save the link, save the image, copy the image, view the image, and cancel the command. You can discover quite a few things by touching and holding on various objects on the PlayBook.

FIGURE 3-3 Touch and hold a URL in the web browser.

DRAG

A *drag* is the combined, sequential motion of touch and hold and swipe. You primarily perform this action on the Home screen when you want to move application icons or designate some for subcategories. When you drag an icon around the Home screen, you can place it in the order you want it to appear and the icon you are dragging will move the icon already in that location to the right or left, depending on what side of the existing icon you release your finger from the moved icon.

PINCH TOGETHER AND APART

When you spread out two fingers in the air, tap the screen with both simultaneously, and then bring them together to meet in the middle; this is considered a *pinch* and will zoom you out on a page. If you perform the opposite and start your fingers together and then pinch them apart, you will zoom in on the page. Pinching is used when viewing photos, surfing with the web browser, working with Word and Excel documents, viewing Bing Maps, and more.

Navigating the Home Screen

You will spend a lot of time on the Home screen of the PlayBook because it is where you launch applications, switch between open applications, view status information, view notifications, and close applications. Now take a walk around the Home screen, starting from the top-left corner:

+ **Notification area**: The notifications area is located in the top left of the PlayBook. You will see a notification icon appear for software updates, new messages, calendar reminders, battery power level, and more. Details on notifications are covered in the next section.

+ **Status bar**: The Status bar is found on the upper part of the display with notifications appearing on the leftmost side of the Status bar, time and date in the center, and a host of status icons and indicators on the right that are described in the next section. The Status bar cannot be hidden on the Home screen.

+ **Minimized applications**: The PlayBook is a multitasking workhorse; therefore, you can have many applications running at the same time. On the Home screen you can find an area below the Status bar and above the remaining application icons in which minimized applications appear in cover-flow form. If there are no open applications, then this area is automatically hidden from view.

+ **Application icons**: Icons for your applications appear on the Home screen in a six-column by three-row layout (in landscape orientation) or four-column by six- row layout (in portrait orientation) that extends down as many pages as needed for all your apps.

Accessing and Reading Notifications

There are two main sections that constitute the notifications area, one is an exclamation point icon and the other indications vary depending on what type of notification has arrived. The exclamation point is used for all notifications and indicates there is a new notification that requests your attention. The various other notification icons let you know what type of notification has arrived and include the following:

+ **Envelope:** This icon indicates you have a new email message (see Figure 3-4).

+ **Check box**: This icon indicates you have a new task due.

+ **Calendar**: This icon indicates you have an appointment reminder.

After you receive a notification, tap the icon to view the specific notification. For example, if you receive a message notification with an Envelope icon, tap the icon to see the latest seven messages (sender, subject, and time). If you tap on a specific message in the list, it opens in the full email program, so you can view and take action on the received message. After you open a message in the email application, the unread count decreases to reflect that you read the new message. If you want to go back to what you were doing before the notification came in, then you simply tap away from the Status bar.

If your PlayBook is connected to a BlackBerry smartphone with a BlackBerry Bridge (see Chapter 5 [How Do I Bridge the PlayBook with My BlackBerry Smartphone?] then you see the upper-left corner of the PlayBook glow red when a new notification is received, like the red flashing light on a BlackBerry (see Figure 3-5). As of this writing, only message and calendar notifications appear this way. The notifications area is accessible by developers but is limited to those applications developed with the native PlayBook SDK.

FIGURE 3-4 Typical messages notification

FIGURE 3-5 Red notification glow

Understanding and Accessing the Status Bar

The Status bar appears at all times on the Home screen, and within applications, and can be toggled on or off by swiping down and up diagonally in the top corners. The left side of the Status bar is where you can find the notifications area, detailed in an earlier section. In the center of the Status bar is the time, date, and alarm indicator (if you have one scheduled). By tapping on this a monthly calendar appears. The right side of the Status bar contains Status bar icons and indicators, including the following:

✦ BlackBerry Bridge toggle and lock controller, as shown in Figure 3-6.

FIGURE 3-6 BB Bridge toggle

✦ Presentation mode indicator when you have the HDMI cable plugged into your PlayBook.

✦ Music controller with a Play or Pause button on the Status bar. After tapping, you see the song details and buttons to Play/Pause, move back, and move forward. This works with the Music app and Podcasts app.

✦ Orientation lock controller with an indicator stating what orientation your PlayBook is currently locked into.

+ Bluetooth connection indicator with a toggle to turn On and Off while showing your active connection.

+ Wi-Fi connection indicator with a toggle to turn On and Off while showing your active connection, as shown in Figure 3-7.

FIGURE 3-7 Wi-Fi connection status

+ Battery indicator that shows the percentage when you tap on it.

+ Gear icon to jump to your PlayBook settings.

Tapping each of these icons, except for the Gear icon, makes a small pop-up appear with more detailed information and toggle switches manipulated by tapping on them.

PORTRAIT ORIENTATION PECULIARITIES In portrait orientation the Status bar gets "squished" so that the BlackBerry Bridge is hidden and half the orientation lock is grayed out. If you tap on the right side of the Status bar, all the icons available appear and you can use them in portrait orientation.

Breaking Down the Menu

The menus in each application, accessed by swiping down from the top of the frame, are all context-sensitive and designed by the PlayBook developer. Take a look at a couple of the common menus found in applications loaded on your PlayBook.

WEB BROWSER

The menu in your web browser is extremely useful, maybe more so than any other menu on your PlayBook. The menu in the browser, as shown in Figure 3-8, is used for the following:

✦ **View open tabs**: You can open up several different browsing session tabs in the web browser, and in the top left and center of the menu you can see thumbnails of these open tabs that you can swipe through and select.

✦ **Open a new tab**: There is a single button to open another browser tab.

✦ **Downloads**: Tap on this icon to enable you to view your download history and active downloads.

✦ **Options**: Tap the Gear icon to open up the browser options. Chapter 4 (How Do I Surf the Web on My PlayBook?) covers these in detail.

FIGURE 3-8 Menu in the web browser

WEATHER

The weather application is provided by `AccuWeather.com` and is preloaded on your PlayBook. The menu in weather, as shown in Figure 3-9, is used for the following:

+ **Toggle between Fahrenheit and Celsius**: Change the temperature scale depending on your preference.

+ **View multiple city weather conditions:** You can view the current day and night forecast for your selected cities and swipe left and right to view other cities you have set up to monitor in the program.

+ **Add or remove cities:** Delete cities that no longer interest you.

FIGURE 3-9 Menu in the weather app

7DIGITAL MUSIC STORE

The PlayBook comes with the 7digital music store, so you can purchase music right from your PlayBook. If you swipe down to reveal the menu you see the following functions, as shown in Figure 3-10:

+ **Store browsing history**: As you browse the music store and tap different album art, the album cover appears on the left and center of the menu area, so you can quickly jump back to these albums.

+ **Featured music**: Tap this icon to see the Featured tab of music.

+ **Options**: Tapping here opens up the basic music store options page.

+ **Help**: Tapping the Help icon actually takes you outside the 7digital music store app to a dedicated help file.

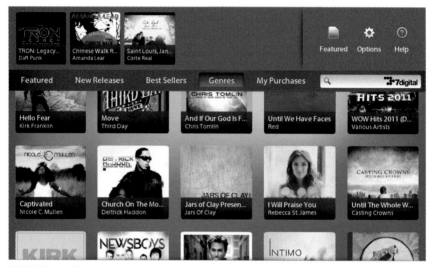

FIGURE 3-10 Menu in the music store

Switching Between Apps

BlackBerry Tablet OS takes multi-tasking seriously, and does so within the way applications function. There are a couple of ways to switch between running applications:

+ **Switch to a minimized app**: Running applications that are minimized appear under the Status bar and above the application launcher in large thumbnails that remain active on the Home screen, (see Figure 3-11). To open a minimized application, simply:

   1. Navigate to the Home screen.

   2. Swipe to the minimized application you want to use.

   3. Tap it to select and open.

Your application remains open and running even if you perform another, unrelated function. For example, if you start a video and then minimize the application because you need to jump to the Home screen, the video continues to play in a small, visible window, even as you flip through other minimized applications on the Home screen (refer to Figure 3-11).

FIGURE 3-11 Minimized applications continue running.

➕ **Switch between running apps**: You can also quickly switch between running applications without minimizing. To do so, swipe your finger left or right within an application to go to the next or previous application. You need to swipe from the frame across the display, and you see the new app display come in slightly smaller and then expand to fill the screen to let you know it is active (see Figure 3-12).

CAN I RUN MANY APPLICATIONS AT ONCE? The OS manages your open applications so an attempt to run more than the device memory can handle at one time results in either the application not opening (requiring you to close one you are not actively using) or dynamically closing an application that is consuming too much memory.

FIGURE 3-12 Switching from video to music via in-app swipe

Using the Keyboard

Unlike the majority of BlackBerry smartphones that have physical QWERTY keyboards, the PlayBook is an all touch screen device, which includes text entry via a pop-up keyboard. The keyboard appears when you tap into a text entry field (see Figure 3-13), or you can activate it by swiping up from the bezel to the display in the bottom-left corner.

FIGURE 3-13 The QWERTY keyboard

The keyboard is a full QWERTY keyboard and works in both landscape and portrait orientations by automatically adjusting the width of each key as the orientation changes. The main keyboard has the following characteristics:

+ All 26 letters of the alphabet
+ Two Shift keys
+ Keyboard minimization key
+ Number/Symbol switch button
+ Localization control so you can choose between the following keyboards:
  + English (US)
  + Spanish
  + English (UK)
  + Dutch
  + French
  + Italian
+ Period key
+ Comma key
+ Backspace key
+ Return button

CAPS LOCK IS AVAILABLE To switch into Caps Lock mode, simply touch and hold on the Shift key and then notice that a blue border forms around the two Shift buttons. Tap once on a Shift key to turn off the Caps Lock.

After pressing the Number/Symbol switch button, you see numbers appear in a phone dialer 3x3 format with 18 more punctuation symbols, as shown in Figure 3-14. There are also two buttons, one on each side of the keyboard, with a blue dot. Tapping this switches to a second symbol keyboard that has 27 more symbols. You can also enter accented and special characters by tapping and holding on different letters of the alphabet, as shown in Figure 3-15. Try different ones out to see what character they activate.

FIGURE 3-14 Numbers on the keyboard

FIGURE 3-15 Accented and special characters

Related Questions

✛ How do I get more apps loaded to switch between and check out their custom menus? **PAGE 216**

✛ How do I bridge my smartphone to see notifications? **PAGE 78**

✛ Where can I read more about the web browser and try out more tabs? **PAGE 60**

CHAPTER FOUR

HOW DO I SURF THE WEB ON MY PLAYBOOK?

In this chapter:

+ Browsing the Web
+ Changing Browser Options
+ Creating and Managing Bookmarks
+ Managing Downloads

One of the primary reasons that people purchase tablet devices is to surf the Web on a larger screen device than their smartphone from the comfort of their favorite chair or couch without having to sit at a desktop or lug around a laptop. The WebKit engine powers the web browser on the BlackBerry PlayBook and is a mobile browser that gets you as close to a full desktop experience as possible with Adobe Flash integration designed right into the browser. Gestures are also supported, so the browsing experience is fun, interactive, and not limited by incompatibilities.

Browsing the Web

By default, your PlayBook's browser is the top-left application icon on the Home screen, under the All tab. There is also a Bridge Browser that appears when you connect your BlackBerry smartphone to your PlayBook, as detailed in Chapter 5 (How Do I Bridge the PlayBook with My BlackBerry Smartphone?). This Bridge browser functions the same as the web browser, but the default settings are different because they require less data and thus are more optimal for a cellular data connection. The Bridge Browser is used when you are away from a Wi-Fi hotspot or if the BlackBerry smartphone 3G/4G cellular data connection you are using is too slow. When you are connected via Wi-Fi you will use the standard browser.

Although the PlayBook did not launch with thousands of applications, the web browser is so powerful and functional that the need for apps such as Twitter, Facebook, Pandora, and more is minimal. RIM includes browser shortcuts on the Home screen for the following websites, complete with custom icons, as shown in Figure 4-1:

+ Gmail
+ Hotmail
+ Yahoo! Mail
+ AOL Mail
+ Facebook
+ Twitter

FIGURE 4-1 Custom browser shortcuts

To access any of these websites, simply tap the selected custom icon right from your PlayBook Home screen. If you want to visit a website from the browser that doesn't already have a short cut, follow these steps:

1. Tap the browser application icon and the web browser opens, showing your bookmarks. (You can change this setting, as discussed in the next section.)

2. Tap a bookmark to visit that website, or tap up in the URL field at the top of the display to enter in a URL. The keyboard appears when you tap in this text entry field.

3. Enter your website URL, and tap Go on the Keyboard. Note a .com key on the keyboard. You do not have to enter http://www because this is auto-filled by the browser. If you enter a website name without a suffix, the text you enter is used with the default search engine, which is another setting you can manage and customize.

- -

TOUCH AND HOLD ON .COM FOR MORE If you touch and hold on the .com button, you see extensions for .net, .org, .edu, .gov, .ca, and .biz, so you can easily add the proper extension when entering the URL you want to visit.

- -

GENERAL NAVIGATION AND BROWSING

While you are at a website, you can perform the following actions:

+ Swipe your finger up, down, left, or right to scroll and pan around the web page.

+ Tap hyperlinks to visit other pages of the site.

+ Spread your fingers apart to zoom in and pinch to zoom out.

+ Double-tap to auto-zoom into columns with text so that you can read the text across the width of the display.

+ Touch and hold on hyperlinks and photos to choose from a number of different functions.

+ Touch and hold on text to select it, and then copy it to the clipboard, as shown in Figure 4-2.

FIGURE 4-2 Copy and paste website text.

+ Swipe down from the top frame to reveal thumbnails of open browser tabs, open a new tab, view downloads, and access the browser options.

+ Tap the button in the upper right of the Status bar to toggle full-screen browsing on and off.

✦ Tap the back or forward arrows located on the upper Status bar to move back a page or forward to a page you have visited.

✦ Tap the open tab browser button on the upper Status bar to view thumbnails of open tabs. This performs a similar action to the swipe down from the frame.

✦ Tap the Clock icon to the right of the URL entry box in the upper Status bar to access your browser history. Tap again to close your browser history.

✦ Tap the gold Star icon in the upper Status bar to access your bookmarks. The next section covers bookmarks in more detail.

✦ Tap the icon to the left of the URL entry field in the upper Status bar to view any certificates associated with the website.

✦ Tap the circular arrow to refresh a page or the X to stop loading the page to the right side of the URL entry field in the upper Status bar.

PORTRAIT BROWSING SUPPORTED, BUT NOT ADVISED It is possible to rotate your PlayBook 90 degrees and browse in portrait orientation, but as you can see in Figure 4-3, the web browsing experience is not optimized for this manner of viewing as you then have to slide right and left to view the upper Status bar and the number of open website tabs shown is very limited.

Examining Tabbed Browsing

Your PlayBook can only open up one session of web browsing at a time, so if you wish to view multiple web pages and move between those pages, you can use the tabbed browsing capability in the PlayBook web browser. As described in the previous section, it is easy to open up a new tab on your PlayBook.

HOW MANY TABS CAN I HAVE OPEN AT THE SAME TIME? You can open tabs until you reach the limit of available memory. I had more than 50 open tabs and three other apps running and still didn't hit the limit.

FIGURE 4-3 Viewing the upper menu in portrait orientation

When the upper menu appears in the browser, you can see up to three and a half thumbnails of open tabs in landscape orientation and two in portrait orientation (see Figure 4-4). To access your other open tabs, simply swipe your finger from right to left to scroll through thumbnail views of the open tabs.

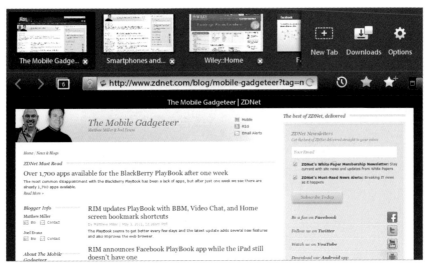

FIGURE 4-4 Open tab thumbnails in landscape view

VIEWING AND MANAGING BROWSER HISTORY

Your browser history can be toggled on and off by tapping the Clock icon with the arrow around it. When you tap to view your history, a display appears with the days on the left and thumbnails of the web pages taking up most of the center and right of the display, as shown in Figure 4-5.

Two icons in the upper right of the history page serve these functions:

➕ **Grid/list icon**: Toggle between grid view and list view.

➕ **Pencil Icon**: Edit your web history with this button by removing individual websites from your browsing history.

The Pencil button simply shows an X (in thumbnail view) or trash can (in list view) that you tap to remove the website from your history (see Figure 4-6). There is no way to edit the title of the page in your history view. The web browser settings, described in the next section, enable you to manage how much of your browsing history is stored and available to you for future access.

FIGURE 4-5 Viewing history in thumbnail mode

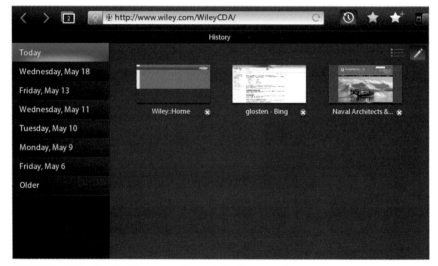

FIGURE 4-6 Tapping the X removes the website from your history

TAP A SECOND TIME TO TOGGLE OFF If you tap either icon to view bookmarks or your browser history, simply tap the icon again to minimize the pages. You can also swipe down from the top frame if you are in full screen mode to switch back to viewing with a top control bar.

Changing Browser Options

The PlayBook web browser is one of the premier functions of the device and RIM gives you the ability to optimize and personalize your browsing experience with browser options. Through the options detailed in this section you will be able to choose your own home page, decide which search engine you want to use, decide which type of content to load, and define your privacy and security settings. As discussed in Chapter 3 (How Do I Navigate My PlayBook?) to access these options, simply swipe down from the top frame to the display to open the web browser's main menu, located at the top of the display. You find the following items in this menu:

+ Thumbnails of open tabs

+ The button for opening a new tab

+ The button to view your downloads

+ The button to access browser options

Tap the Gear icon located on the far right of the main menu to launch a page that shows you four categories on the left: General, Content, Permissions, and Privacy & Security. Each category contains several options you can change to customize your PlayBook browsing experience. Notice the Back button in the upper left to take you back out of the web browser options.

GENERAL

Seven options are available on the General settings page, as shown in Figure 4-7:

+ **For a New Page Show**: Select what will appear by default when you open up a new tab. Your two choices are My Bookmarks or My Home Page.

+ **Home Page**: Choose your home page and enter the website URL (the default is `http://us.blackberry.com`).

+ **Search Engine**: Pick your preferred search engine from the list of Bing, Google, Yahoo, and AOL. This will be what your browser uses to search for keywords you type in the URL field.

+ **Remember Open Tabs When I Start Browser**: Toggle this feature On if you open a large number of the same tabs on a regular basis. When turned on, every time you launch the browser those same tabs that you had open when you quit your last browsing session will automatically open up and for you.

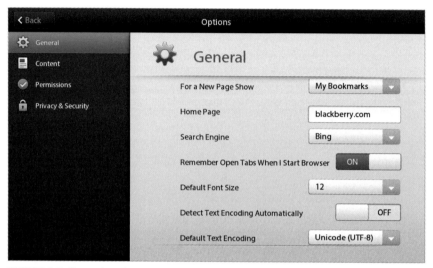

FIGURE 4-7 General settings page

✤ **Default Font Size**: Control how large the font is on the display to make readability match your preference. Font choices range from 9 to 120.

✤ **Default Text Encoding Automatically**: The PlayBook web browser picks up the text encoding for sites automatically by default, but here you have the option to turn this off and then select a text encoding option for yourself.

✤ **Default Text Encoding**: If you turn off text encoding, then a drop-down list will be activated here for you to choose from a number of encoding options, including Western (Macintosh), Japanese (Shift_JIS) and many more. By default, Unicode (UTF-8) is selected and is likely where most people will leave the setting.

CONTENT

The Content options page contains three toggles that enable you to slide between On and Off; all are in the On position by default (see Figure 4-8). The content toggles in the PlayBook web browser control include the following:

✤ Load Images

✤ Enable Flash

✤ Enable Javascript

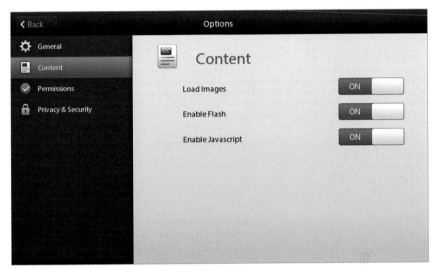

FIGURE 4-8 Content options

Although this is a simple options area, these three options have a significant impact on the speed and responsiveness of your browser experience. If you have Flash enabled, you may see performance slow down because Flash is resource heavy and demands a lot from your PlayBook as content loads. Image loading and Javascript support can also slow down the browsing experience a bit, but they make for a richer web browsing experience. These can be important considerations if you connect primarily through your smartphone where data speeds are not as fast as a Wi-Fi network.

PERMISSIONS

You have a single toggle controller for On or Off in the permissions options area, as shown Figure 4-9. Here you can toggle the capability to allow websites to access your location. If you use location-based social networking sites, such as Foursquare, or mapping sites, such as Google Maps, you want to enable this setting in the browser.

After turning on this permission and visiting a site that accesses your location, your location appears in the list of domains that try to determine where you are located. You can tap on the Pencil icon to open up the screen to select Allow or Deny access to your location for a specific domain.

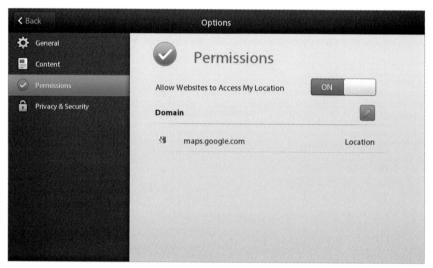

FIGURE 4-9   Permissions options

PRIVACY & SECURITY

Six options are available for you to manage your privacy and security with another five quick access buttons to clear various caches.

These six options include the following, as shown in Figure 4-10:

✦ **Keep History For**: Choose how long your PlayBook stores your browsing history. Options are available for 1 to 30 days.

✦ **Private browsing**: Turn this on to ensure that, no history, cookies, or any other browsing history data is stored on your PlayBook.

✦ **Block Pop-ups**: Turn this on or off to manage pop-ups.

✦ **Accept Cookies**: A cookie is a piece of text stored by a web browser used for authentication, storing site preferences, shopping cart contents, the identifier for a server-based session, or anything else that can be accomplished through storing text data. Turn this option on to speed up browsing since these cookies maintain your preferences each time you return to a site. Cookies can be used to track activity, so if you are concerned with security you may want to turn this option off.

FIGURE 4-10 Six options in Privacy & Security

+ **Enable Websockets**: Websockets is a communications technology that improves directional communications over the transmission control protocol (TCP) socket. Turn this on or off to manage your connection protocol. The default is set to off because the technology is still in development and there are some security concerns with it.

+ **Enable Web Inspector**: Web Inspector is a function available in Webkit-based browsers and turning this on gives web developers full access to site details such as the page source, script debugging, HTML and JavaScript properties, and more. The default is set to off, but if you want it on, set up a password on your PlayBook to turn on the Web Inspector toggle.

Additionally, there are five one tap buttons to clear information at the bottom of the Privacy & Security page and include the following, as shown in Figure 4-11:

+ **Clear History**: This option clears out all of your web browser history. The ability to view your history was described earlier in this chapter.

+ **Clear Cache**: Select this option to clear out temporary internet files such as images, sounds, web pages, and more. It is a good idea to clear this from time-to-time as extensive web browsing will build up a cache that consumes some of your internal storage capacity.

+ **Clear Cookies**: Select this option to clear out the cookies mentioned earlier that are also stored for a period of time. Similar to clearing your cache, you may want to clear these out periodically to keep your internal storage clear.

+ **Clear Local Storage**: Local storage, also known as Document Object Mode (DOM) storage, is similar to cookies, but cookies are limited to about 4 KB of data while local storage can be larger. Again, select this option from time to time to keep your browser storage needs down to a manageable level.

+ **Clear All**: This button allows you to clear all four of the preceding areas at one time.

All the settings that you enable or disable on these four pages are saved as you toggle the switches or make your selections. Simply tap on the Back button in the upper-left corner to return to surfing the Web in the web browser and your settings will be saved.

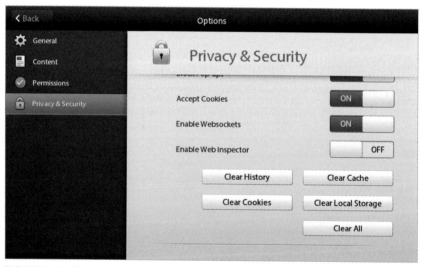

FIGURE 4-11 Clear buttons

Creating and Managing Bookmarks

One of the fastest ways to surf the Web on your BlackBerry PlayBook is by simply tapping bookmarks and jumping right to your favorite websites. There are two important controls in your browser tool bar that can help you do this. These tools include:

- **Gold Star**: Located in the upper control bar, use this icon to view your bookmarks page.

- **Star with Green Plus**: Use this icon to add the page you are viewing to your bookmarks page.

These two tools simplify the process of adding and finding bookmarks. The following steps describe how to use them together to save and view a web page:

1. After visiting a website you want to save as a bookmark to access later, tap the star with green +. A small pop-up appears in the upper right.

2. Tap the Add to Bookmarks option.

3. Then, to find and access this bookmark later, tap the gold star; you can see thumbnails of your bookmarked web pages in a grid, as shown in Figure 4-12. If you add more than 12 bookmarks, the thumbnails appear below the viewable screen, so you need to scroll up to see more bookmarks.

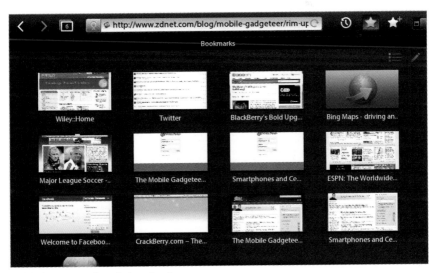

FIGURE 4-12 Bookmark thumbnails

You can also tap on the List icon in the upper right to see all your book-marks in a list view with a small icon, site name, and URL. You can delete bookmarks by tapping the Pencil icon and then tapping the X or Trash Can icon, the same as the way you delete pages in your history.

The BlackBerry Tablet OS update 1.0.3.1868, released in early May 2011, added the ability to tap the star with the green + and choose to add the page you are viewing to your Home screen. To add a website to your Home screen, follow these steps:

1. Visit a site you want to add to your Home screen; then tap the star with green +. A small pop-up appears in the upper right (see Figure 4-13).

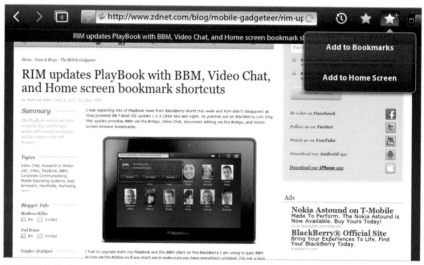

FIGURE 4-13 Pop-up to add to Home screen

2. Tap the option to Add to Home Screen. Another pop-up appears with a small thumbnail and a text entry field for the site name. You can tap the site name and edit it as you want (see Figure 4-14).

3. Tap the Save button, and your shortcut is added to your Home screen where you can move it around as you want.

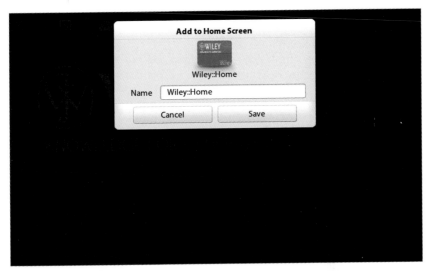

FIGURE 4-14 Edit the site name.

CREATE A BETTER LOOKING HOME SCREEN ICON By default, the PlayBook captures the viewable screen of the site being bookmarked and stores that image as the Home screen icon for the site you selected. If you find the screen capture too small to distinguish on your Home screen, you can simply use the pinch gesture to zoom in so that the screen capture creates a usable screen icon.

Managing Downloads

The PlayBook web browser enables you to download files, videos, images, and other items, whether or not you can actually install them. Testing this capability reveals there are no restrictions on size or type of file that you can download, but you can view or use files that are supported only by the BlackBerry Tablet OS. After you select a link to download a file, the download begins and completes in the background. To check on your downloads, perform the following steps:

1. Swipe from the upper frame down to the viewable display to open the upper menu.

2. Tap Downloads. A page opens showing your active downloads.

3. Tap a downloaded object to open it up in a supported application. Supported files to download include:

   + Images

   + Videos

   + Music

   + Word and Excel documents

   + PDF files

Files that you may download that are not supported through apps on the device remain in the Downloads folder. You can delete them by tapping the X icon and you can transfer them to your computer using your USB cable or Wi-Fi connection as detailed in Chapters 10 (How Can I View, Share, and Capture Pictures on My PlayBook?) and 15 (How Do I Manage My PlayBook with BlackBerry Desktop Software?).

Related Questions

+ How do I connect to a network so that I can use the web browser through Wi-Fi? **PAGE 21**

+ How do I check out pictures I download from the Internet? **PAGE 191**

+ What can I do with the Office files I download via the web browser? **PAGE 122**

CHAPTER FIVE

HOW DO I BRIDGE THE PLAYBOOK WITH MY BLACKBERRY SMARTPHONE?

In this chapter:

+ Set Up the Bridge via Bluetooth
+ Accessing and Using Bridge Files
+ Browsing the Web through the Bridge Browser
+ Using BlackBerry Messenger (BBM) through the Bridge

Because RIM values security, the PlayBook requires a BlackBerry smart-phone for email, contacts, calendar, memos, tasks, and BlackBerry Messenger usage, connected via a utility called BlackBerry Bridge. Thus, there is no personal or corporate data related to these applications stored on the actual PlayBook device. You can also browse files stored on your smartphone and even save them from your PlayBook directly to your BlackBerry phone. The Bridge connection gives you the ability to use the web browser through your smartphone data connection so you can browse when you are outside the range of a Wi-Fi hotspot.

Set Up the Bridge via Bluetooth

One of the initial steps in the setup process is to connect your BlackBerry smartphone to your PlayBook, detailed in Chapter 2 (How Do I Set Up and Customize My PlayBook?) If you did not perform this connection during the setup process or need to change your connection to another BlackBerry smartphone, follow these steps:

1. Tap the Settings icon (gear shape) in the upper-right corner and choose BlackBerry Bridge from the list of options on the left.

2. Tap the Setup button in the lower-right corner of the display that appears (see Figure 5-1). This takes you to a screen asking for the name of your PlayBook.

3. You can change the name for your PlayBook here or leave it the same as it appears. Tap the Next button to proceed.

4. Tap the Install Now button to initiate the installation process for BlackBerry Bridge on your smartphone. This process is described in detail in Chapter 2.

5. After you have BlackBerry Bridge installed on your smartphone, tap the Continue button at the bottom center of the display and follow the instructions to scan the barcode and connect your PlayBook to your BlackBerry smartphone, as shown in Figure 5-2. You can also tap on the Manual Pairing button and follow the steps to make the connection without using the barcode.

6. After a successful pairing is made, you will see a success confirmation screen with a button to tap for Done (see Figure 5-3).

FIGURE 5-1 BlackBerry Bridge setup start screen

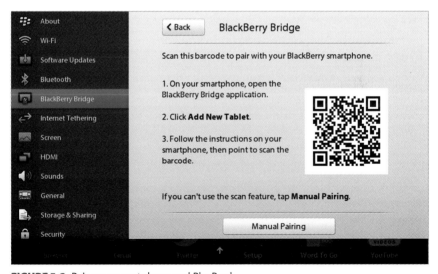

FIGURE 5-2 Pair your smartphone and PlayBook.

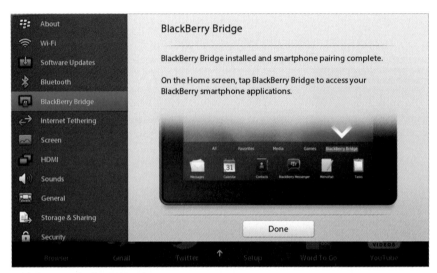

FIGURE 5-3 Confirmation of success

Chapter 6 (How Can I Read and Use Email on My PlayBook?) and Chapter 7 (How Can I Hone My Organizational Skills Using My PlayBook?) cover specific details on using email, calendar, tasks, and memos. The following sections cover the other Bridge functions.

Accessing and Using Bridge Files

Your BlackBerry smartphone enables you to send and receive email attachments, capture photos and videos, and enjoy music. With a Bridge connection and the Bridge files utility, you can extend these experiences to the large screen of the PlayBook and you can access Word, Excel, and PDF files stored on your smartphone with full editing capabilities, rather than having to peer into a much smaller smartphone display. Many BlackBerry smartphones come with the standard version of Documents To Go preloaded, so you can view documents only, with no support for document creation. With a BlackBerry smartphone connected to your PlayBook through the BlackBerry Bridge you can do a lot more in this program, including the following:

✦ Create a document or spreadsheet and save it to your smartphone, (see Figure 5-4) or send it via email.

✦ Open a document or spreadsheet saved on your smartphone, maybe something you received as an attachment, and then save it to the large internal storage area of your PlayBook.

SAVE TO YOUR SMARTPHONE OR PLAYBOOK When you save documents in Documents to Go, you can choose to save either to your PlayBook or bridged smartphone from within the application.

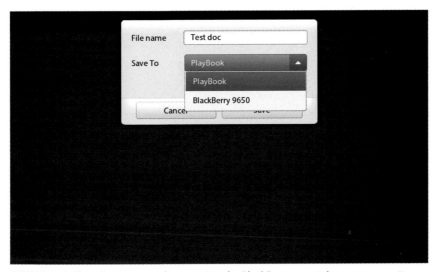

FIGURE 5-4 Choosing to save a document to the BlackBerry smartphone

---

MEDIA SUPPORT THROUGH FILES IS COMING As of this writing, there is no support for pictures, videos, or music in the Bridge Files utility. Support will be enabled on the PlayBook with software updates.

To use Bridge Files and open documents on either of your bridged devices, follow these steps:

1. Tap the BlackBerry Bridge tab on the Home screen.

2. Tap the Bridge Files icon from the BlackBerry Bridge tab. The Bridge Files utility opens with a switch at the top to toggle between your BlackBerry smartphone and PlayBook.

3. Find a file you want to open, tap the file, and then tap the Open button at the bottom center of the display (see Figure 5-5). The file opens in the applicable application.

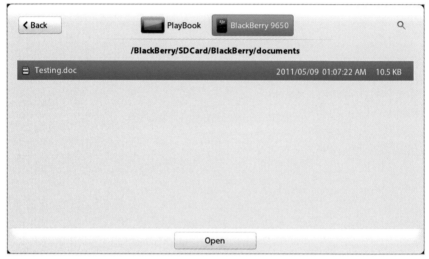

FIGURE 5-5 Viewing files on the BlackBerry smartphone

Browsing the Web through the Bridge Browser

As of this writing, the only BlackBerry PlayBook model available for purchase is the Wi-Fi-only model. These Wi-Fi models require you to have a means to connect to the Internet via Wi-Fi. However, for those of you with a BlackBerry smartphone, RIM added a bonus feature that enables you to connect to the Internet via Bluetooth to your smartphone for browsing through the Bridge Browser. Therefore, you don't need to be connected to a Wi-Fi network to browse the Internet. You can make this Bluetooth connection and surf the

Web anywhere you want without incurring carrier tethering charges like you will if you turn your smartphone into a portable Wi-Fi hotspot.

WILL BRIDGE BROWSING BE SLOWER THAN WI-FI? Connections made through the Bridge are usually slower than a Wi-Fi connection to a wired Internet access point.

APPEARS THE SAME, BUT THEY ARE DIFFERENT Although the default and bridged web browsers appear to be the same, if you launch the default web browser from the Home screen while connected only via the BlackBerry Bridge to your BlackBerry smartphone, you will receive a network error. You can browse the Web only through the Bridge Browser when you connect in this manner. Shortcuts on your Home screen do not work in the Bridge Browser either.

To enjoy the Internet on your PlayBook through your bridged BlackBerry smartphone, follow these steps:

1. Tap the BlackBerry Bridge tab on the Home screen.

2. Tap the Bridge Browser icon. The web browser detailed in Chapter 4 (How Do I Surf the Web on My PlayBook?) appears (see Figure 5-6). Some of the web browser settings are set to different defaults to help reduce the amount of memory required to surf via this Bluetooth tethered connection.

ADD BRIDGE BROWSER AS A FAVORITE Don't forget that you can simply drag and drop the Bridge Browser icon onto your Favorites tab on the Home screen to get faster access to it when you connect to your smartphone.

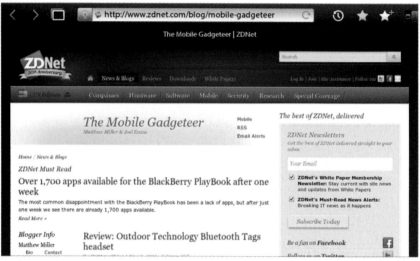

FIGURE 5-6 Browsing through the Bridge Browser

NO HOME SCREEN BOOKMARKS SHORTCUTS WHEN BRIDGED
Another minor difference between this browser and the full browser is the lack of functionality to add bookmarks to the Home screen as shortcuts. Tapping the Add Bookmark icon (white star with green plus) adds the site as a bookmark but does not give you the option to add this site as a shortcut, like you see in the full web browser.

Using BlackBerry Messenger (BBM) through the Bridge

A function rolled out with the 1.0.3.1868 update during BlackBerry World 2011 that supports BlackBerry Messenger through a Bridge connection. BBM through the Bridge functions like email, calendar, tasks, and other apps in which everything is mirrored on the PlayBook via Bluetooth while all data remains on the smartphone. To use BBM on your PlayBook, follow these steps:

1. Tap the BlackBerry Bridge tab on the Home screen.

2. Tap the BBM icon. Open chat sessions, and your contact list appears on the display (see Figure 5-7). Whatever was active on your smartphone appears on the PlayBook display.

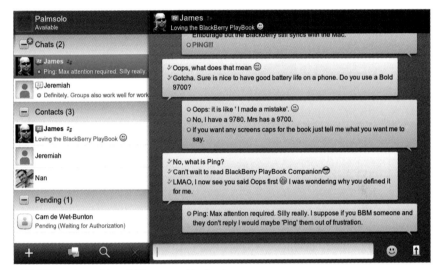

FIGURE 5-7 Launching BBM on your PlayBook

3. Tap a contact name, and then enter text in the text entry field to chat with your friend. Use emoticons by tapping the Happy Face icon and pinging, invite a friend to a group chat, or add an attachment to the chat by tapping on the up arrow in the bottom-right corner, as shown in Figure 5-8.

4. You can also tap the following icons in the bottom action bar:

   ✚ Tap the white + to send an invite to someone's PIN, email address, or name to add him as a BBM friend.

   ✚ Tap the multicolor Bubble icon to start a group chat. A pop-up appears where you can select friends to add to the chat session (see Figure 5-9).

   ✚ Tap the Magnifying Glass icon to search for friends in your BBM contact list (see Figure 5-10).

   ✚ Tap the red X to end a chat session or remove someone from your contact list. There is a confirmation prior to an action being taken.

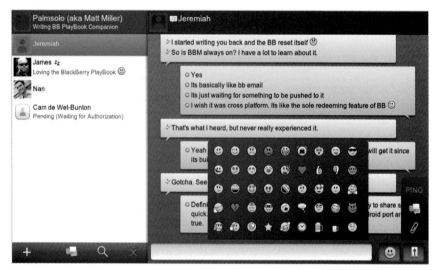

FIGURE 5-8 Available options when chatting with your friend

FIGURE 5-9 Initiating a group chat session

TOGGLE THE SEARCH AND END BUTTONS To turn off the Search function or End function (to end the chat/remove someone from the chat), simply tap the magnifying glass or red X a second time.

FIGURE 5-10 Conducting a search

You can also manage your own BBM profile from your PlayBook. Tap your name in the upper-left corner, and your profile appears, as shown in Figure 5-11.

FIGURE 5-11 Managing your profile on the PlayBook

You can view or edit the following in your BBM profile from your PlayBook:

+ **Profile photo**: Simply tap it and choose a photo on your PlayBook or BlackBerry smartphone to use for your profile picture.

+ **Display name**: Tap the space to the right of the label, and enter the name you want to display.

+ **Personal message**: Tap the space, and enter a message that appears under your display name in BBM.

+ **Status**: Tap the drop-down arrow to select from Available or Busy.

+ **PIN**: Your PIN is visible, so you can easily find it and share it with others.

+ **PIN Barcode**: The QR code is presented on your display, so you can show it to friends to have them scan it in to add you to their contact list.

BRIDGE AUTO STARTS WHEN YOU INITIATE A CONNECTION After a period of time (controlled in your settings) with no activity by you on the device, the PlayBook goes into standby mode. To reconnect via the Bridge, tap on one of the Bridge apps, such as BBM, and the connection is made automatically as the application opens up to where you last were.

Related Questions

+ Can I do more with a tethered BlackBerry smartphone than just browse the Web? **PAGE 263**

+ What do I do if I can't get the Bridge to work? **PAGE 292**

+ How do I toggle the keyboard in BBM? **PAGE 54**

CHAPTER SIX

HOW CAN I READ AND USE EMAIL ON MY PLAYBOOK?

In this chapter:

+ Using Email through the Bridge
+ Using Email through the Browser

The PlayBook launched with security as a focus, and as a result there are only two methods to use email on the device: through the BlackBerry Bridge from your BlackBerry smartphone and through the web browser. A standalone email client will subsequently launch to give those who don't have a BlackBerry smartphone or those who don't want to use a web browser capability to access their email, but has yet to appear on the market. The two methods available as of this writing are excellent methods for reading and composing email messages, and as a bonus, ensure that email remains out of the hands of strangers who may find or steal a PlayBook from someone.

Using Email through the Bridge

The optimal email experience on the PlayBook is through the Bridge because the BlackBerry Bridge extends the smartphone email experience to a large display. Email is presented in the Messages utility on the PlayBook. This is different than Messages on BlackBerry smartphones where email, text messages, BBM posts, Twitter posts, and Facebook status updates all appear in a single user interface. To access and read your email via a BlackBerry Bridge connection, follow these steps:

1. Tap the BlackBerry Bridge tab on the Home screen.

2. Tap the Messages icon. In landscape orientation, the Messages utility opens with email messages from all the email accounts you have set up on your BlackBerry smartphone, appearing in a list in the left column, as shown in Figure 6-1. The top message appears highlighted with a preview panel of the email taking up about two-thirds of the display. In portrait orientation, the email messages appear with sender name, subject, and time stamp of the message (see Figure 6-2.)

3. Tap an email to select it and read it on your PlayBook.

FILTER BY ACCOUNT You can tap the drop-down arrow to the right of All Messages and then select one of your email accounts to filter your inbox to just view emails from one selected account. You can also select a specific folder from within an account to view email in that folder.

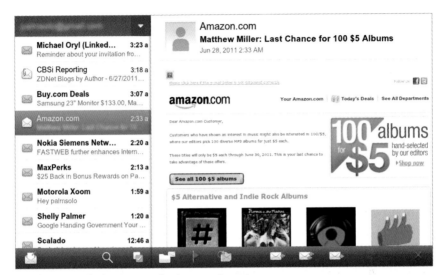

FIGURE 6-1 Default Messages landscape orientation

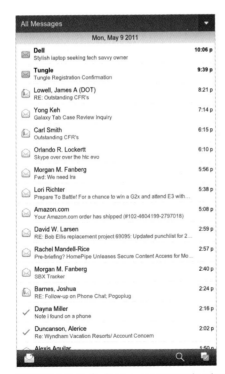

FIGURE 6-2 Default Messages portrait orientation

Seven controls display at the bottom of each open email to manage actions you can take with that email message, including the following:

	Move	Click this icon to move a message to a selected folder. Folders are present for Inbox, Spam, and Outbox (see Figure 6-3).
	Flag	Click this icon to flag a message and then select options for request (11 responses to choose from), color (7 colors to choose from), status (completed or not completed), and add a due date, as shown in Figure 6-4.
	Mark as Read/ Unread	Click this icon to toggle a message between read and unread status. The sender of the email changes to bold font when you toggle a message to unread status.
	Reply	When you select this option an email composition page opens up with the sender in the recipient box. Enter the body of the email to finish and then tap on send.
	Reply All	When you select this option an email composition page opens up with all parties who received the original email appearing in the recipient box. Enter the body of the email to finish and then tap on send.
	Forward	Use this option to send an email you received to someone who was not an original recipient or to one of those recipients with your own comments.
	Delete	The red X is used to delete a message and after tapping on it you see a confirmation pop-up appear to confirm your intended action.

WHAT'S BEEN READ? Email with closed yellow envelopes and bold font face sender email addresses indicate the message is unread. After you read the message, the envelope top opens up, the envelope turns white, and there is no longer any bold font used, as shown in Figure 6-5.

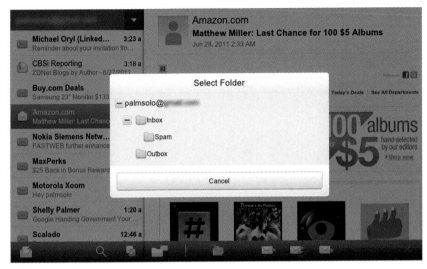

FIGURE 6-3 Move to a selected folder.

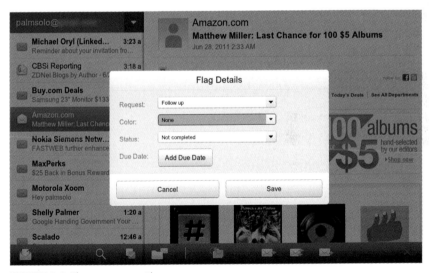

FIGURE 6-4 Flag message options

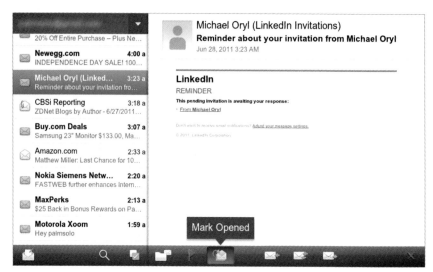

FIGURE 6-5 Toggling a message between read and unread

In portrait orientation, a circular arrow icon appears on the far left (see Figure 6-6) that closes the open email message and takes you back to the inbox view.

FIGURE 6-6 Circular arrow icon in far left

FIGURE 6-7 Attachments appear at the top of your email.

The following three icons appear under the email list view on the left third
of the viewable screen:

- **Open envelope with pen:** Compose a new email.
- **Magnifying glass:** Search through your email.
- **Blue check box:** Use the Multi-email check box toggle button to turn
  on a check box in front of email messages, so you can batch move or
  delete messages in your inbox.

FIGURE 6-8 Search field options

When you choose to compose a new email, enter or select the following (see Figure 6-9):

1. Use the drop-down selector to choose the email account to send from.

2. Enter a recipient and CC or BCC recipients.

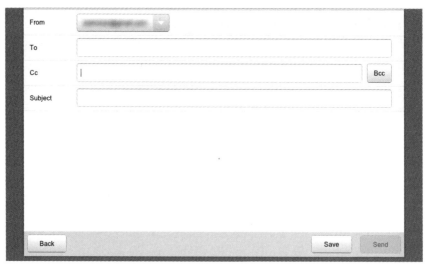

FIGURE 6-9 Composing a new email

3. Enter a subject.

4. Enter the body of your email.

5. Select high or low priority, flag details (same as mentioned earlier), and decide if you want to add an attachment or not.

AUTO FILTER AS YOU TYPE In the recipient fields, your contact list is auto-filtered as you enter letters to more quickly add recipients to your new email.

Using Email through the Browser

If you do not have a BlackBerry smartphone, you can try using email through the PlayBook's web browser. By default, RIM includes custom icon web browser shortcuts to the following email websites, as shown in Figure 6-10:

+ Gmail

+ Hotmail

+ Yahoo! Mail

+ AOL Mail

FIGURE 6-10 Custom web browser email shortcuts

Thus, you can simply tap one of these icons to go to the website to log in and use your preferred online email client.

BE CAREFUL IF YOU DELETE A CUSTOM EMAIL ICON RIM included some cool icons on the device, but if you don't have an email account with a particular client and want to remove that icon, you can. However, you cannot add that icon back without a full wipe and reboot, so make sure you actually do want to delete it.

The Gmail email view is optimized for the 7.7 inch display (see Figure 6-11); you can find buttons in places that optimize the viewable area and give you the feel that you have a native client. For example, you can view next and previous emails in your inbox by tapping the arrows in the bottom-right corner, as shown in Figure 6-12. There is a drop-down arrow with options for the following, as shown in Figures 6-13:

+ Reply
+ Move
+ Label
+ Mute
+ Report Spam
+ Print
+ Mark as Unread/Read

ARE THERE LIMITS TO ACCESSING EMAIL FROM THE BROWSER? Yes, various limits exist if you choose to access your email via the web browser. For instance, when accessing Gmail through your PlayBook's web browser, there is no way to add an attachment, receive a notification, or use the print option.

FIGURE 6-11 Typical view of Gmail in the web browser

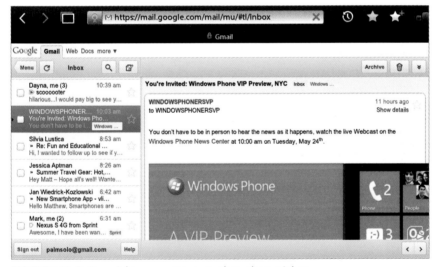

FIGURE 6-12 Bottom right arrows move you through your inbox.

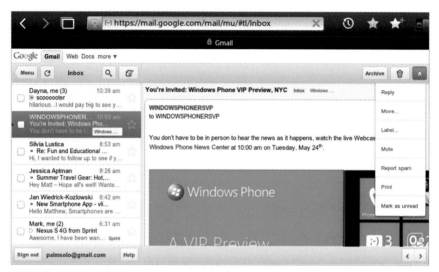

FIGURE 6-13 Drop-down arrow options in landscape orientation

WHERE IS THE STAND-ALONE EMAIL APPLICATION? RIM plans to release dedicated email and PIM apps (contacts, calendar, tasks, memos) in late-2011. The dedicated email application on the PlayBook will enable users to set up email accounts through POP or IMAP with a user interface that closely matches what you find when you use the BlackBerry Bridge with your smartphone. No BlackBerry smartphone is needed to send and receive emails using this dedicated email client.

Related Questions

✦ What apps are used to view the attachments I receive? **PAGE 122**

✦ How do I Bridge my smartphone to access my email? **PAGE 78**

✦ Where can I read more about the web browser and how it works? **PAGE 60**

CHAPTER SEVEN

HOW CAN I HONE MY ORGANIZATIONAL SKILLS USING MY PLAYBOOK?

In this chapter:

+ View Your Calendar
+ Create a New Appointment
+ Manage Contacts
+ Create and View Tasks
+ Create and View Memos
+ Record Voice Notes

ersonal information management (PIM) includes accessing your calendar, contacts, tasks, and memos to manage your daily life. Most of these functions are used on your PlayBook through the BlackBerry Bridge to your BlackBerry smartphone, thus keeping all your PIM data secure and in a centralized location. The PlayBook gives you the ability to view your data in a larger format and in many cases, makes it easier to create new appointments, add new contacts, manage your tasks, and create new text and voice notes.

View Your Calendar

The Calendar application is only available on your PlayBook after you connect your BlackBerry smartphone via BlackBerry Bridge. As you can see in Figure 7-1, it is one of the application icons that appear on the BlackBerry Bridge Home screen tab. To access your calendar, simply tap on the Calendar application icon.

FIGURE 7-1 BlackBerry Bridge Home screen tab

Your calendar opens in the last calendar view you were in when you closed the application. You can find three icons at the bottom center of your calendar that enable you to toggle between these views:

+ Day view

+ Week view (see Figure 7-2)

+ Month view (see Figure 7-3)

WHICH ICON SHOWS WHICH VIEW? Look at the green shading on each of the three icons to determine which one is the day, week, or month view. You can also touch and hold on each icon, and the name for it pops up.

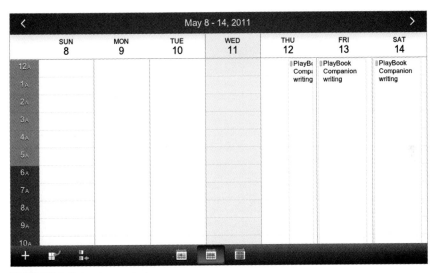

FIGURE 7-2 Calendar week view

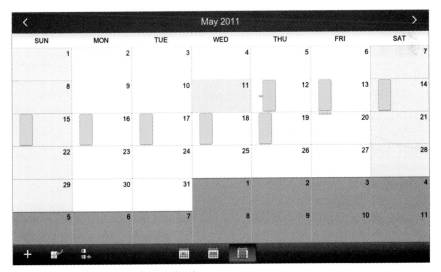

FIGURE 7-3 Calendar month view, landscape

The arrows in the top bar of each of these views enable you to quickly move forward or back one day, one week, or one month at a time. If you want to quickly jump to a different day, follow these steps:

1. Tap the Go to Date button, the second icon in from the left in the bottom toolbar (touch and hold on the icon to see its name). A monthly calendar pops up over the top of your existing calendar view (see Figure 7-4).

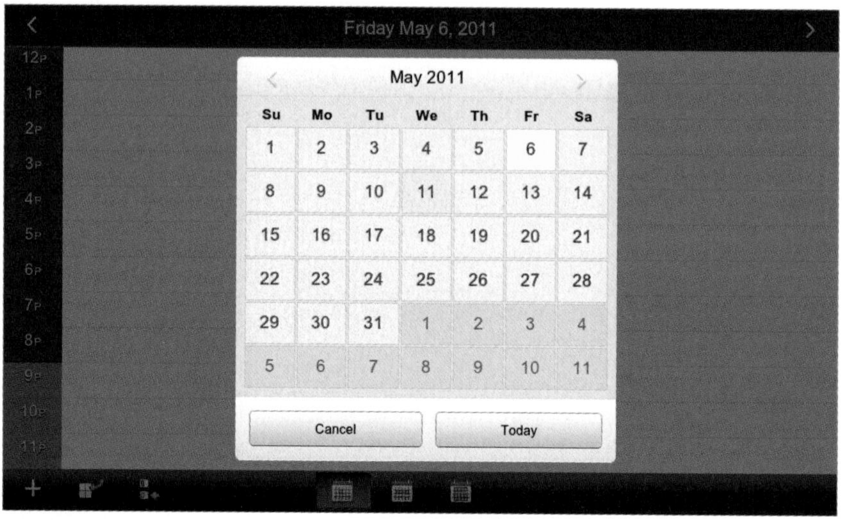

FIGURE 7-4 Go to Date pop-up selector

2. Tap on a day you want to view. You can use the arrows on the top to jump back and forward one month at a time. You can also tap the Today button. Note that the current date is highlighted in blue whereas the day you are currently viewing, if different, is highlighted in yellow.

Because the PlayBook Calendar simply mirrors your BlackBerry smartphone calendar, you also have the ability to view calendars from multiple sources. Thus, you can view an Exchange calendar, one from Google, one from Facebook, and so on. Calendars can only be added or removed from your BlackBerry smartphone. To filter calendar services on your PlayBook, follow these steps:

1. With your Calendar open, tap the Calendar Services button, the third icon in from the left in the bottom toolbar. A pop-up appears over the top of your existing calendar view (see Figure 7-5).

2. Tap the check box next to the calendars you want to include in your view on the PlayBook.

3. Tap the Done button to accept the filter change.

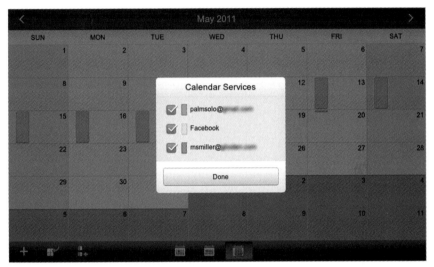

FIGURE 7-5 Calendar Services selector

To view the details for a specific appointment, find one on your calendar and tap it. Details for the appointment appear on the right side of your display in landscape orientation (see Figure 7-6) or in a balloon pop-up in portrait orientation.

- -

DIFFERENT COLORS FOR DIFFERENT CALENDAR SERVICES RIM assigns different colors to the different calendar services you have on your devices. If you forget what color is assigned to which service, simply tap the Calendar Services button to see the designations again.

- -

RIM announced it would release standalone applications for PIM functions that do not require a BlackBerry smartphone connected through the BlackBerry Bridge, but as of this writing, these apps are not yet available. One third-party solution that offers basic calendar viewing functions without the need for a BlackBerry smartphone is Tungle (www.tungle.me). Acquired by Rim in April 2011, Tungle is a free, online scheduling service that syncs with several calendar providers including Outlook, Google Calendar, iCal/Entourage, Lotus Notes, Windows Live, and Yahoo! Calendar. The free Tungle downloadable application for the PlayBook is only a viewer that shows your calendar in a weekly view (see Figure 7-7). You do not have any ability to add or edit appointments using the Tungle application.

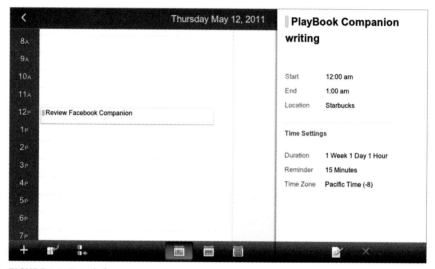

FIGURE 7-6 Details for your appointment

FIGURE 7-7 Tungle calendar view

Create a New Appointment

In addition to viewing your calendar, you can create appointments on your PlayBook if you have a BlackBerry smartphone connected via the BlackBerry Bridge. The user interface for creating an appointment is optimized for the large touch screen display on the PlayBook. To create a new appointment, follow these steps:

1. Tap the Calendar application icon to open up your calendar and tap the + icon in the bottom left, identified as the New Appointment button. A display appears with several drop-down lists, text entry fields, and check boxes for you to use to define your new appointment.

2. Tap the drop-down to the right of the Calendar line and select which one of your calendar services you want to use to create the new appointment, as shown in Figure 7-8.

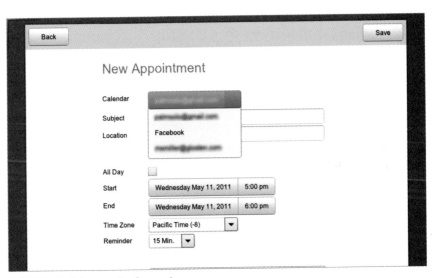

FIGURE 7-8 Select a calendar service.

3. Enter text for the subject and location of the appointment in the next two lines.

4. Define the appointment time using the following selectors:

+ All day toggle.

+ Start and end day and time selectors.

+ Select your time zone.

+ Select a reminder time (None, 0, 5, 10, 15, 30, or 45 minutes up to 1 week options).

5. Enter names of attendees. As you start entering text for a name, you see your contact list filtered so that you can easily select people to invite to your appointment.

6. Establish recurrence settings and select an end date with the following daily, weekly, monthly, and yearly options:

+ **Daily**: Enter the number of days that the appointment will take.

+ **Weekly**: Choose what weeks it occurs on (every week, every other, and so on) and what days it happens on (Sunday through Saturday).

+ **Monthly**: Choose which day of the month it happens on and how often.

7. Enter any notes you want to include in your new appointment and tap the Save button to save your new appointment.

If you added attendees to your new appointment, then after you save your new appointment, invitations are sent out to them automatically via the associated calendar service you selected.

- -

SAVE A FEW STEPS TO CREATE A NEW APPOINTMENT If you are already in the day or week view, tap a day and then tap again on a certain time to create an appointment with a start time for the hour on which you tapped (see Figure 7-9). After the second tap the new appointment page appears with the start and end dates auto-filled in, based on where you tapped on the display.

- -

FIGURE 7-9 Quick appointment entry tap

Manage Contacts

In addition to your calendar, Contacts is a major PIM function that you can manage on your PlayBook. You need a BlackBerry smartphone connected via the BlackBerry Bridge to access and manage your contacts.

VIEW YOUR CONTACTS

To view your contacts, simply tap on the Contacts application icon. Contacts launches by showing you the first contact in your contact database. The layout for Contacts in landscape orientation is as follows (shown in Figure 7-10):

+ **Left side**: This area shows letters in order from A to Z in index form, so you can quickly tap one and jump to that area of your contact database.

+ **Left of center**: Look here to see the contact photo, name, and company of your contacts; you can see up to eight contacts at one time. This is the area where you tap on a contact to select them.

+ **Right side**: Here you can find the contact card showing all available details for your selected contact. Details include name, company, email, address, phone numbers, notes, and more.

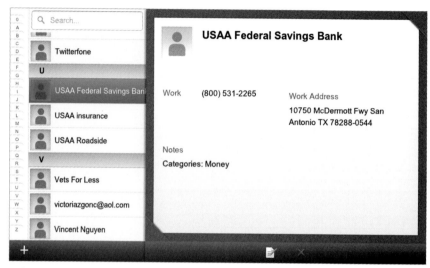

FIGURE 7-10 Typical contact view in landscape

When you rotate your PlayBook into portrait orientation, you can see the left side index and the list of your contacts expands to show up to 15 at one time.

EDIT OR DELETE YOUR CONTACTS

Two icons in the bottom right of your Contacts applications enable you to edit your contacts:

- **Pen and paper**: Tap this Edit icon to view and edit the contact details, as shown in Figure 7-11, which is what you see when you create a new contact.
- **Red X**: Tap this Delete icon and a confirmation pop-up appears for you to confirm your intention to delete that contact. You can also tap the Delete button from the Edit Contact screen (refer to Figure 7-11).

CREATE A NEW CONTACT

You can add new contacts directly on your PlayBook when your BlackBerry smartphone is connected through the Bridge. To create a new contact, tap on the + icon in the bottom left of your Contacts application display. A new contact card appears with the text entry fields shown in Figures 7-12 and 7-13.

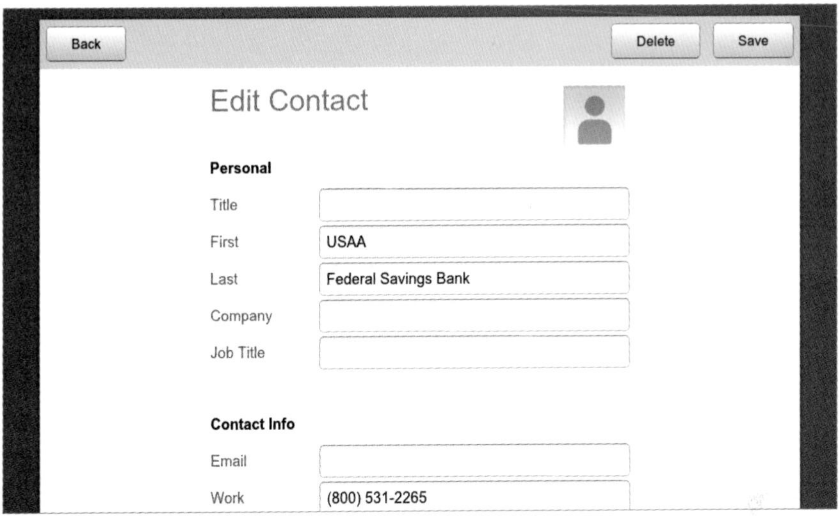

FIGURE 7-11 Editing a contact

FIGURE 7-12 Personal and Contact Info

FIGURE 7-13 Work and home address data

AUTOMATIC LINK CREATION If you enter an email address or website for your contact, after creation you see that the BlackBerry Tablet OS turns these into hyperlinks, so tapping on them launches the email application or web browser and performs the intended actions. Unlike your BlackBerry smartphone, phone numbers are not linked because the PlayBook is not capable of making phone calls.

Create and View Tasks

Although you can create an appointment and use that as a to-do list, it is easier to maintain and manage tasks using an application dedicated for such actions. With a BlackBerry smartphone connected via the BlackBerry Bridge, you can access the Tasks application. Tap on the Tasks icon to launch Tasks. In landscape orientation you see your list of tasks on the left and details for the selected task on the right, as shown in Figure 7-14. In portrait orientation, you can find just a list of your tasks; you need to tap on one to open a page showing all the details.

FIGURE 7-14 Tasks in landscape

ICONS IN TASKS As you can see to the left of each task name, (refer to Figure 7-14), different icons indicate various levels of importance and status. High is a red exclamation, normal has no icon, and low importance has a blue down arrow. Different icons also appear for each of the five status levels.

To create a new task, follow these steps:

1. Tap the +icon in the lower left of the Tasks application and a new task page appears. Enter the name of your task.

2. Tap the arrow to select your task status, as shown in Figure 7-15. Options for status include the following:

   + Not Started
   + In Progress
   + Completed
   + Waiting
   + Deferred

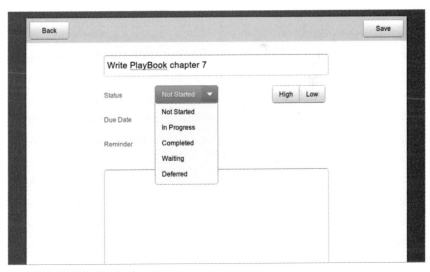

FIGURE 7-15 Selecting task status

3. Select the importance using the High or Low buttons; normal is selected by default.

4. Select a due date, including a recurrence, and enter notes for the task. These can include specific lists, such as Christmas shopping lists.

5. Tap the Save button to save your new task. View full, new task creation options in Figure 7-16.

Similar to the way that appointments and contacts are managed, you can tap the Edit or Delete icon to take these actions on tasks. For quicker access to find a task among many, you can also search through your tasks by simply tapping into the search box in the upper left and entering a search term. Your search is limited to filtering only the first letter of a task name.

FIGURE 7-16 New task creation in portrait orientation

REMINDERS NOT SUPPORTED ON THE PLAYBOOK Although you can see Reminder button when you create a new task on your PlayBook, this is only available on the BlackBerry smartphone, so tapping it just shows you a notice.

Create and View Memos

A memo or note is a handy way to collect your thoughts and create lists that are not dependent on dates or completion status. The Memos interface is similar to the Tasks interface, as you can see in Figure 7-17.

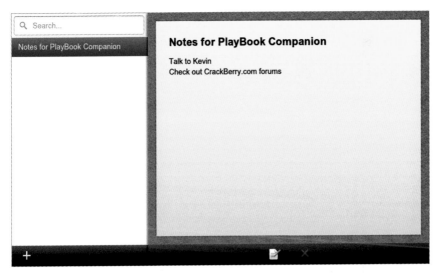

FIGURE 7-17 Memos in landscape

To create a new memo, follow these steps:

1. Tap the +icon after launching Memos.

2. Enter a title for your note on the line labeled New Memo.

3. Enter text into the body of the memo, as shown in Figure 7-18.

4. Tap the Save button to save the memo.

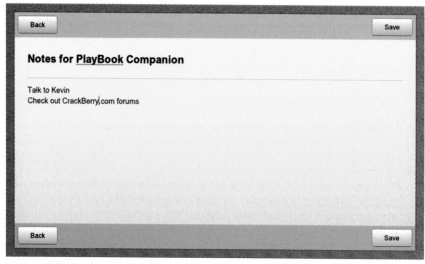

FIGURE 7-18 Creating a new memo

Similar to the way that you manage appointments and tasks, you can tap the Edit or Delete icon to take these actions on memos. For quicker access to find a memo among many, you can also search through your memos by simply tapping into the search box in the upper left and entering a search term. Your search is limited to filtering only the first letter of a memo name.

Record Voice Notes

If you are on the go and don't have time to create text-based memos or tasks, you may want to consider creating voice notes. The Voice Notes application on your PlayBook is a standalone application that does not require you to have a BlackBerry smartphone or be connected via the BlackBerry Bridge.

To create a voice note, follow these steps:

1. From your Home screen, tap the Voice Notes icon.

2. Tap the red circle record button (see Figure 7-19).

3. Speak to record your voice note. You can tap the Pause Button (pair of vertical parallel lines icon) to pause during a recording and then tap the Record button again to continue recording to that same voice note file (see Figure 7-20).

FIGURE 7-19 Tap to record.

FIGURE 7-20 Recording a voice note

4. Tap the square icon to stop recording. After you press Stop, the PlayBook automatically saves your voice note, which appears with a date/time stamp in the list of your voice notes. There is no way to edit the name of the voice note.

AUDIO RECORDING LEVELS Notice as your record your voice note the green to red meter below the Record button fluctuates with your voice. This gives you an indication as to the volume level of the note you record.

To listen to a voice note, simply tap on the note you want to hear in the list of notes. You can move forward or backward within a voice note as you listen to it by tapping on the blue playback indicator that shows where you are currently in the recording (see Figure 7-21).

VOICE NOTE TIME LIMIT AND APPROXIMATE FILE SIZE After tapping Record, you can record a voice note for as long as you want or until you reach your storage capacity limit. BlackBerry smartphones are limited to recording notes up to 1 hour each. Voice notes are recorded at fairly high-quality 128 kbps and consume about 1MB for each minute of recording.

FIGURE 7-21 Listening to a voice note

To delete a voice note, follow these steps:

1. From within the Voice Notes applications, swipe your finger from the top frame down to the display to open up your top menu.

2. Tap the Edit icon. A blue check box appears to the right of each voice note.

3. Tap the check boxes next to the note you want to delete.

4. Tap the trash can icon to remove the notes. A confirmation pop-up appears for you to confirm your intended action, as shown in Figure 7-22.

5. Tap the Cancel button or swipe again to close the upper menu.

MULTITASKING SUPPORTS RECORDING AS YOU DO OTHER THINGS
With the fantastic multitasking capability of the PlayBook, you can start a recording and then work with other apps while your recording continues in the background.

FIGURE 7-22 Deleting voice notes

Related Questions

✦ How do I Bridge my smartphone to get access to PIM data? **PAGE 78**

✦ Where can I find more apps for PIM functions? **PAGE 216**

✦ How can I back up my recorded voice notes? **PAGE 284**

CHAPTER EIGHT

HOW CAN I CREATE, EDIT, AND VIEW OFFICE FILES ON MY PLAYBOOK?

In this chapter:

+ Using Word To Go
+ Using Sheet To Go
+ Using Slideshow To Go
+ Viewing PDF Files

DataViz developed the popular Documents To Go Office suite that BlackBerry, iOS, Symbian, Palm, and Android mobile devices have used for years. In September 2010, RIM acquired DataViz, and its Documents To Go suite is now integrated into the BlackBerry PlayBook to provide native Word and Excel viewing, editing, and creation functionality with PowerPoint and Adobe PDF viewing capability. With this native Office support, you can get work done on the go, use the PlayBook to give presentations, and show off documents on a large display via HDMI output.

Using Word To Go

DataViz's powerful word processor module in the Documents To Go suite, Word To Go, fully supports Microsoft Office files, including the latest Office 2010 suite with Word documents that have a `.docx` extension. DataViz integrates its InTact Technology into Documents To Go so that the original formatting and layout of your document is maintained. Even though the PlayBook display doesn't currently support some data such as headers, footers, and footnotes, it does store and save that information, enabling you to still edit the document on your PlayBook; then, when you send it to someone or transfer it to your PC, all original data that was hidden from you on the PlayBook is restored. This technology enables you to use your PlayBook for editing without worrying about destroying advanced formatting of the original document.

VIEWING DOCUMENTS

Viewing documents in Word To Go sent via email is an easy process. Follow these steps to download and view:

1. Open up an email with a supported Word attachment.
2. Tap the attachment to download it, as shown in Figure 8-1. The file starts downloading, and the download status appears in your email.
3. The document attachment automatically opens up in Word To Go on your PlayBook (see Figure 8-2).

SHOULD I USE PORTRAIT OR LANDSCAPE? The Word To Go experience is available in portrait view but optimized for landscape view.

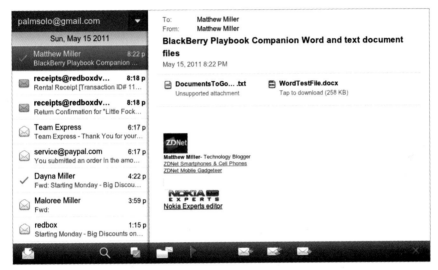

FIGURE 8-1 Email with text file attachments

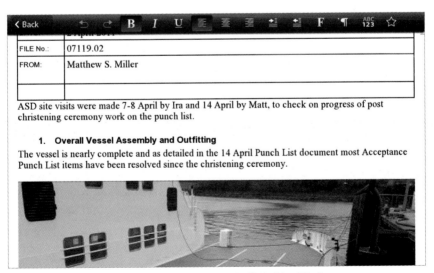

FIGURE 8-2 Word attachment opens up automatically in Word To Go.

NO SUPPORT FOR .TXT FILES Word To Go on the PlayBook supports only Word documents, so if you receive a text file with a `.txt` or `.rtf` extension, it will not download from within an email to your PlayBook. The text below the attachment states, "Unsupported attachment."

You can also transfer documents to your PlayBook through a desktop connection via USB. To transfer a document via USB and view it on your PlayBook, follow these steps:

1. Connect your PlayBook with the USB cable to your PC or Mac.

2. Find a file you want to transfer, and then click and drag it over to the Documents folder found on your connected PlayBook's directory structure. You cannot place the file into the root directory; if you try to do this, a security error pop-up appears.

3. Disconnect your PlayBook from your computer and tap on the Word To Go icon to launch the application.

4. Tap on the Browse button (see Figure 8-3) and in the PlayBook browser window tap the Documents tab.

5. Tap the file you want to open (see Figure 8-4) and then tap the Open button, and the file opens in Word To Go.

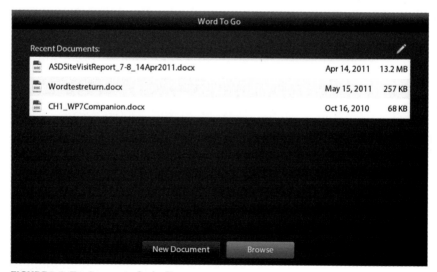

FIGURE 8-3 Tap Browse to find a file to open.

FIGURE 8-4 Tap a file to open it in Word To Go.

- -

FILE LIMIT IN EMAIL, NOT IN USB TRANSFER There is a 2.9MB attachment limitation in the BlackBerry 6 smartphone operating system, so files larger than this cannot download to your PlayBook via the BlackBerry Bridge. Word To Go opens files of any size, so if you want to view files larger than this, you must transfer them to your PlayBook via USB where there is no file size limit.

- -

CREATING AND EDITING DOCUMENTS

Although Word To Go is not equivalent to Microsoft Word on your desktop, it is a capable mobile client that enables you to write text and add basic formatting to your document. Follow these steps to create a new document:

1. Tap the Word To Go icon to launch the application.

2. Tap the New Document button to create a new Word document (see Figure 8-5). Word To Go opens up a blank new document with the keyboard available for you to start entering text.

FIGURE 8-5 Tap the New Document button to start a new document.

PINCH TO ZOOM You can control the zoom levels in Word To Go and Sheet To Go by using the two-finger pinch apart (zoom in) or pinch together (zoom out) technique explained in Chapter 3 (How Do I Navigate My PlayBook?).

Now that you have a blank new document page open on the PlayBook, look at what the buttons in the top bar are used for, working from left to right:

- **Undo arrow**: Press to undo last action and repeat to undo the action before the previous one. Repeat to continue.

- **Redo arrow**: Press to redo or bring back the last action that you undid. Repeatedly tap this to return as far as to where you began to undo.

- **Bold (B):** Tap to make all future text bold font or to change selected text to bold font.

- **Italic (I):** Tap to italicize all future text or to change selected text into italics.

- **Underline (U):** Tap to underline all future text or to change selected text to be underlined.

- **Left alignment**: Aligns text to the left side of the page.
- **Center alignment**: Places text in the center of the page.
- **Right alignment**: Aligns text to the right side of the page.
- **Right indent**: Indents text on the line where you have the cursor to the default tab location to the right. Press repeatedly to move indentation further to the right.
- **Left indent**: Moves the indentation to the left one tab at a time. Press repeatedly to move indentation further to the left.
- **Font style (F)**: Tap to see this Font Style pop-up menu appear (see Figure 8-6).

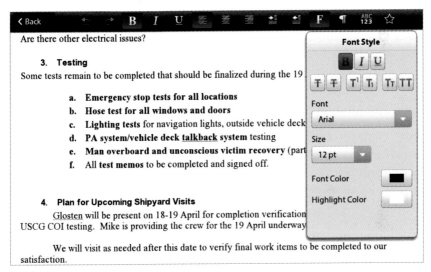

FIGURE 8-6 Font style options

- **Paragraph formatting**: There is a wide selection of paragraph formats, (see Figure 8-7) that you can apply to the paragraph where the cursor is located or to a block of selected text.
- **Document word count:** Counts words, characters, and paragraphs.
- **Bookmarks (star)**: After tapping the star icon and viewing the bookmarks pop-up window, tap the + to add a bookmark and the X to remove a bookmark.

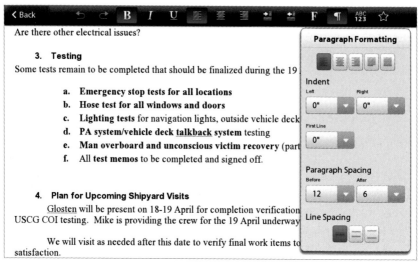

FIGURE 8-7 Paragraph formatting pop-up

MISSING SOME BASIC FORMATTING Although Word To Go has several formatting and alignment options, RIM is currently missing a few formatting areas, including any type of list support (bullets, numbers, outline), picture insertion, or table entry. However, if you open an existing document that already has lists, you can add onto it by pressing the return key at the end of the last entry.

To edit text in a document, follow these steps:

1. Tap where you want to begin your selection and the cursor appears with a long, blue Bar icon beneath it.

2. Touch and hold on the blue Bar icon, and a pop-up appears with options to Select Text or Cancel (see Figure 8-8).

3. Tap the Select Text icon and a second Blue Bar icon appears.

4. Touch and hold either or both icons and drag them to select the text you want to edit.

5. Tap Cut or Copy to perform these actions. If you want to apply formatting to the selected text, tap the document outside the pop-up; then tap on the Format icon you want to apply to this text (see Figure 8-9).

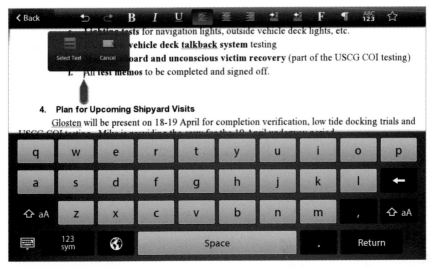

FIGURE 8-8 Selection options

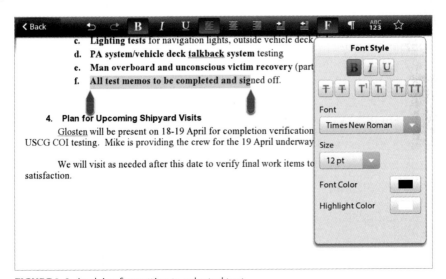

FIGURE 8-9 Applying formatting to selected text

As you enter text, you may see a red underline appear under misspelled words. This is the automatic spell checker feature in Word To Go. If you tap on the word underlined in red, the correct spelling suggestions appear, as shown in Figure 8-10; tap on one to select it and insert the correct word.

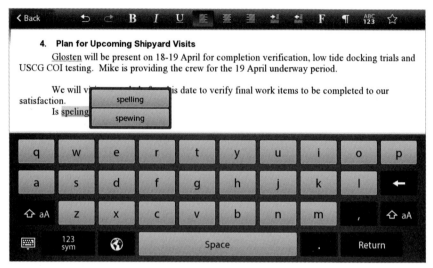

FIGURE 8-10 Spelling suggestions

After you finish creating a new document or editing an existing one, you need to save it. To do so, follow these instructions:

1. Slide your finger down from the upper frame to the display to open the top menu bar, as shown in Figure 8-11.

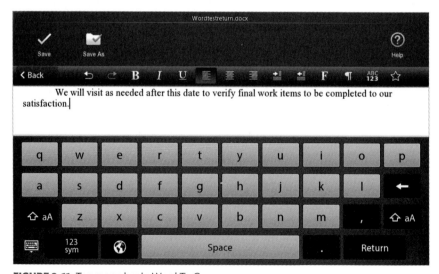

FIGURE 8-11 Top menu bar in Word To Go

2. From here you can select to Save or Save As. Tap Save to save the document with the same name and location as when you opened it; if you tap on Save As a pop-up appears with options to enter a filename and a choice to save it to your PlayBook or BlackBerry smartphone (if you have an active BlackBerry Bridge connection).

3. Tap on the Back button to go back to the main Word To Go Home screen or simply jump to another application or the PlayBook Home screen if you want. If you have not yet saved your document when you press the Back button, a pop-up appears prompting you to choose to Discard, Save, or Save As. Choose one to continue.

WHAT FORMAT ARE DOCUMENTS SAVED IN? If you create a new document and then save it on your PlayBook, the document will be saved with a `.doc` extension by default. If you open up an existing Word document with a `.docx` extension, when you choose to save, it will be saved with that same `.docx` extension. There is no option for selecting the specific Word format your document is saved with on the PlayBook.

Using Sheet To Go

Like Word To Go, you can use Sheet To Go as a standalone application or in combination with a BlackBerry Bridge connected to your smartphone that enables you to access attachments and save workbooks directly to your BlackBerry smartphone. Sheet To Go is a good start for a spreadsheet program, but there is a lot of work to do to make it as useful as the Word To Go application. Some major limitations include the following:

+ No copy and paste capability for cells
+ No formula/function list to help you figure out what you want to use
+ No ability to resize rows or columns, so text longer than the default cell width is hidden when you have something in an adjacent cell
+ No filtering or sorting of rows
+ No support for graphs

VIEWING SPREADSHEETS

It is likely that the majority of the time you spend with Sheet To Go is used for viewing spreadsheets that you receive via email on your PlayBook. Even if you just want to view a spreadsheet you receive, DataViz and RIM include the full Documents To Go suite so that you can actually edit it after opening. Follow these steps to view a spreadsheet attached in an email:

1. Open up an email with a supported Excel attachment and tap the attachment to download it; as it downloads the download status appears in your email.

2. The spreadsheet attachment opens up automatically in Sheet To Go on your PlayBook.

You can view Sheet To Go spreadsheets in portrait or landscape orientation, but the experience is optimized for landscape. In portrait orientation you have to slide the toolbar icons from right to left to view all of them.

NO SUPPORT FOR .CSV FILES Sheet To Go on the PlayBook supports only Excel spreadsheets, so if you receive an attachment or copy of a file in some other format, you won't be able to download it from within an email to your PlayBook or view it in the file browser as a supported spreadsheet.

You can also transfer spreadsheets to your PlayBook through a desktop connection via USB. To transfer a spreadsheet via USB and view it on your PlayBook, follow these steps:

1. Connect your PlayBook with the USB cable to your PC or Mac.

2. Find a file you want to transfer, and then click and drag it over to the Documents folder found on your connected PlayBook's directory structure. Do not place the file into the root directory though; if you try, a security error pop-up appears.

3. Disconnect your PlayBook from your computer.

4. Tap the Sheet To Go icon to launch the application.

5. Tap the Browse button and then tap on the Documents tab.

6. Tap the file you want to open and then tap the Open button to view the file in Sheet To Go.

CREATING AND EDITING SPREADSHEETS

Although Sheet To Go is not equivalent to Microsoft Excel on your desktop, it is a decent mobile client that enables you to create basic spreadsheets. Editing spreadsheets functions the same as new spreadsheet creations do.

Follow these steps to create a new spreadsheet:

1. Tap the Sheet To Go icon to launch the application.

2. Tap the New Document button to create a new Excel document. Sheet To Go opens up a blank new spreadsheet with cell A1 selected, as shown in Figure 8-12.

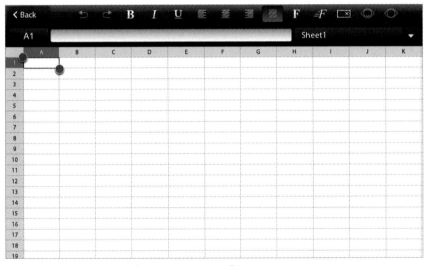

FIGURE 8-12 A new spreadsheet starts out in cell A1.

Now that you have a blank new spreadsheet open on the PlayBook, take a look at the buttons in the top menu bar. These buttons function the same as the ones in Word To Go with only a few exceptions. Working from left to right, the exceptions are:

+ **Justified text**: Aligns the text along both edges of the cell.

+ **Font style (F)**: Number and font styles are available in Sheet To Go in the pop-up menu that appears when you tap the F button, as shown in Figure 8-13.

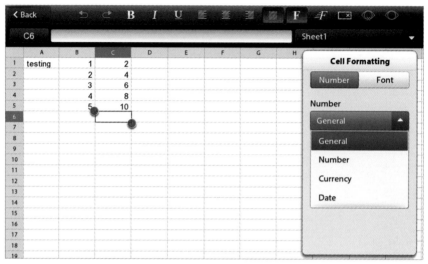

FIGURE 8-13 Cell formatting options

The following number styles are available to apply to the selected cell(s):

+ **Custom**: Choose your own format.

+ **General**: No specific format.

+ **Number**: Select comma for 1000, negative number format, and decimal places to show (0–30 available).

+ **Currency**: Select currency type, negative number format, and decimal places.

+ **Date**: Select from a multitude of date formats.

+ **Time**: Select from a multitude of time formats.

+ **Percentage**: Select the number of decimal places.

+ **Scientific**: Select the number of decimal places.

+ **Text**: Use for cells when only text is desired, even if there are numbers in the text field.

The following font styles are available to apply to the selected cell(s):

+ **Bold**

+ **Italics**

+ **Underline**

- **Left align**
- **Center align**
- **Right align**
- **Font Style**: Extensive list of fonts
- **Font Size**: 6 through 72 point available
- **Font Color**: 16 colors available
- **Fill Color**: 16 colors available
- **Word wrap toggle**
- **Quick Format options**: The Quick Format pop-up, as shown in Figure 8-14, enables you tap on one format option that can change your selected cell(s) to the most common format for that particular type of data. Quick Format options include the following:
    - **Number**: Formats numbers to 2 decimal places
    - **Time**: Formats to 0:00 format
    - **Percentage**: Formats cell(s) to a percent with 2 decimal places
    - **Text**: Simply changes content to standard text
    - **Currency**: Formats data to $1.00 format
    - **Date**: Formats data to month/day format

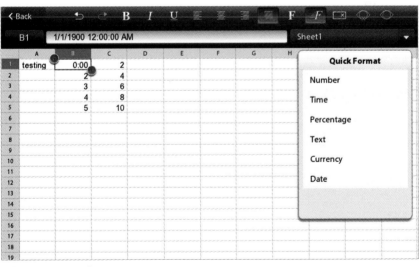

FIGURE 8-14 Quick Format pop-up

The last three options, unique to Sheet To Go, are located in the upper right corner and are as follows:

+ **Clear cell(s):** This box with an X icon clears text from selected cell(s).
+ **Hide cell(s)**: This eyeball with an X icon hides selected rows or columns from view.
+ **Show cell(s):** This clear eyeball icon shows hidden rows or columns.

Below the upper menu toolbar you can find the cell editing bar with the cell identifier, cell entry field, and sheet selector drop-down. If you tap the cell identifier, you can jump to any cell in the spreadsheet.

- -

HIDE AND SHOW TIPS To hide cells in rows or columns, select those rows or columns and then tap the Eye with the X icon. To show the hidden cells, use the row/column selectors and select those rows or columns to either side of the hidden rows or columns; then tap the Eye icon in the upper right.

- -

Now that you know what the upper toolbar and cell editing bar are used for, you can edit a spreadsheet by following these steps:

1. Tap a cell you want to enter data or formulas into.

2. Tap into the cell editing block below the main toolbar. The upper toolbar will be minimized while the keyboard appears for text and data entry, as shown Figure 8-15.

3. Enter in numbers, formulas, or text. Be sure to enter an equals sign to start a formula.

4. Tap on return or the check mark to enter the cell data into the spreadsheet and move to another cell. You can also tap on the X mark to close out of the cell entry function. Tapping the X on the far right of the entry block clears out the specific cell.

5. Tap the sheet selector drop-down to jump between multiple spreadsheets within your workbook file.

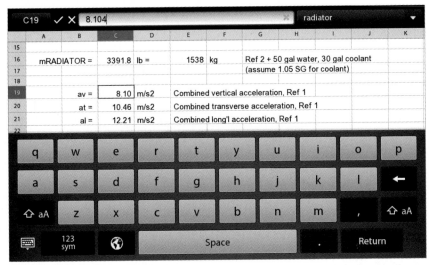

FIGURE 8-15 Entering data into a cell

SEE MORE OF YOUR SPREADSHEET If the keyboard is getting in the way while you try to see some of your spreadsheet during cell creation, tap the Keyboard icon in the bottom-left corner to minimize it. Tapping again in the cell editing block brings the keyboard back up for continued data entry.

FORMULA ASSIST Sheet To Go has a large number of formulas integrated into the program. Although there is no formula selector, you can enter a known formula name, such as SUM, along with a first parenthesis. A yellow pop-up appears to help you choose the correct format of arguments to enter into your formula, as shown in Figure 8-16. Try out some of your most used formulas to see if Sheet To Go provides them.

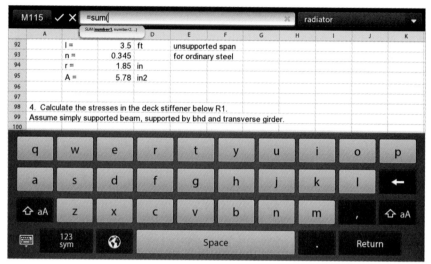

FIGURE 8-16 Formula assist pop-up

DATA LINKING BETWEEN SHEETS You can enter formulas to connect data between spreadsheets within a workbook. To link a cell in one sheet with another, use the common Excel syntax:

`='OtherSheetName'!SpecificCellinOtherSheet`

and you see the data work well between spreadsheets in your workbook.

You can perform some of these text manipulation functions within a selected cell by following these steps:

1. Tap and hold on the data in the cell editing block of the cell you want to edit. A pop-up appears, as shown in Figure 8-17, with options for cut, copy, paste, delete, and select.

2. Tap one of these buttons to perform the intended action and then tap on a cell where you want to paste in this data if applicable.

3. A bug in the Sheet To Go program requires you to first enter any character in the cell editing block (for example a letter m) to paste in the copied data. Touch and hold on this character and select paste.

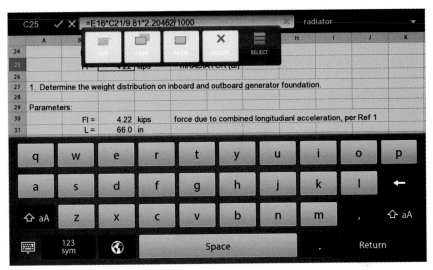

FIGURE 8-17 Cut, copy, paste options

WHAT FORMAT ARE SPREADSHEETS SAVED IN? If you create a new spreadsheet and save it on your PlayBook, the document will be saved with an `.xls` extension by default. If you open an existing Excel document with an `.xlsx` extension, it will maintain that same `.xlsx` extension when you save. There is no option to choose which Excel format to save your spreadsheet with on the PlayBook.

Using Slideshow To Go

Although Word To Go and Sheet To Go both enable you to view, edit, and create documents, Slideshow To Go only enables viewing PowerPoint files, and functions only in landscape orientation. Over time, DataViz added PowerPoint editing and creation to iOS and Android clients, so Slideshow To Go may eventually support these capabilities, but as of this writing it is not editable.

VIEWING PRESENTATIONS

To view a presentation you first need to get a presentation onto your PlayBook. You can do so by either opening one attached to an email or transferring one via USB cable. Follow the same steps detailed earlier in the Word To Go and Sheet To Go sections to get a PowerPoint file loaded on your PlayBook in one of these two ways. PowerPoint files with .ppt and .pptx file extensions are supported on the BlackBerry PlayBook. After finding a file and opening it up, some controls appear at the top of the page, as shown in Figure 8-18.

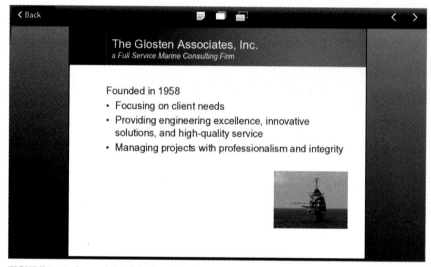

FIGURE 8-18 Controls in Slideshow To Go

These buttons control the following (from left to right):

✦ **Back**: This button returns to the main Presentation To Go Home screen.

✦ **Notes**: Tap this toggle to see your presentation notes at the bottom of the display (see Figure 8-19).

✦ **Slide sorter**: Tap this center toggle icon to see all your slides in the left side of the display as thumbnails, (see Figure 8-20).

✦ **Presenter mode**: This toggle requires that you connect your HDMI cable to your PlayBook and an external display to enable presenter mode, as discussed in the following section.

✦ **Back and forward**: Tap these arrows to move through the slides in your presentation.

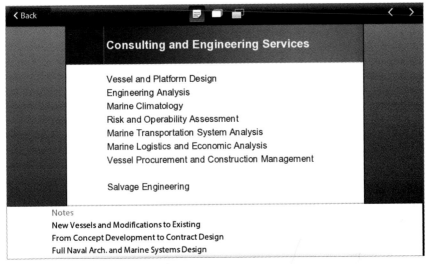

FIGURE 8-19 Notes appear at the bottom.

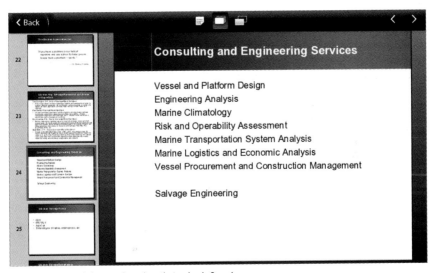

FIGURE 8-20 Slides as thumbnails in the left column

YOU CAN REARRANGE YOUR SLIDESHOW One basic editing feature supported is the ability to reorder your slides. With the slide sorter toggle enabled, you can simply touch and hold on a slide and then drag it to a new location within your slideshow. You can then save this new PowerPoint file for future use in this new order.

GIVING A PRESENTATION VIA YOUR PLAYBOOK

After selecting a PowerPoint file to use for your presentation and reordering any slides you want to move around, connect your PlayBook to an external display through the HDMI out connection port. The full display of your PlayBook appears on the external display, but to ensure a better presentation experience, tap the third icon to the right to enable presenter mode. The following benefits are available in presenter mode, as compared to just showing Slideshow To Go:

✦ Slide numbers appear on your PlayBook display but not on the external display.

✦ Notes appear on the PlayBook display but not on the external display.

✦ No upper toolbar or menu bar appears on the external display.

✦ If you enable slide sorter view it appears on your PlayBook but not on the external display.

NO ZOOMING IN PRESENTER MODE Two-finger zoom gestures are disabled in presenter mode. You can only navigate between slides using a single finger swipe motion when this mode is enabled and you are connected to an external display.

Viewing PDF Files

DataViz has a PDF To Go module on other mobile platforms, but on the PlayBook you find a basic Adobe Reader client provided directly by Adobe. To view PDF files on your PlayBook, you can download them from an attachment or transfer them via the USB cable, as mentioned earlier in this chapter. If a PDF file comes through email, it opens automatically after you download it. If you transfer a PDF file to your PlayBook or have an older email attachment stored on your PlayBook that you want to view, follow these steps:

1. Tap the Adobe Reader icon to launch the application.

2. Find a PDF file stored on your PlayBook or BlackBerry smartphone, if connected via the BlackBerry Bridge.

3. Tap the Open button. You can view it in landscape or portrait orientation. You can use your two-finger gestures to zoom in and out; a double-tap toggles between default zoom levels.

NAVIGATE QUICKLY THROUGH A PDF DOCUMENT Although you can swipe your finger right and left across the display to scroll through your pages, it is faster to use the scroll bar for navigating through many pages at once. Simply slide down the menu from the top, tap on the square in the bottom slider bar, slide your finger left and right to navigate to your desired page, and then lift up your finger to go to that page (see Figure 8-21).

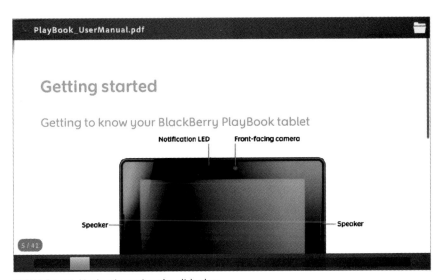

FIGURE 8-21 Navigating using the slider bar

To close the PDF file you are viewing and access another, perform the following actions:

1. Slide down from the top frame to the display to reveal the menu, as shown in Figure 8-22.

2. Tap the file folder icon on the far right.

3. Follow steps 2 and 3 in the previous list to open another PDF file.

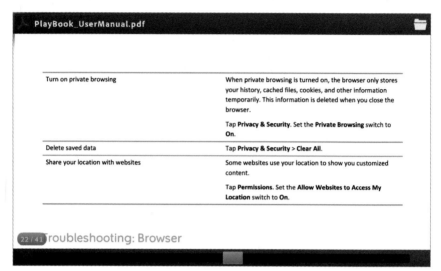

FIGURE 8-22 Slide down to reveal top menu.

Related Questions

+ How do I perform gestures to pan and zoom in my files? **PAGES 43 AND 45**

+ How do I bridge my smartphone to access my email? **PAGE 78**

+ Can I listen to music as I work in a Word or Excel file? **PAGE 146**

CHAPTER NINE

HOW DO I ENJOY MUSIC AND VIDEO ON MY PLAYBOOK?

In this chapter:

+ Enjoying Music Loaded onto Your PlayBook

+ Browsing and Purchasing Music through the 7digital Music Store

+ Listening to Music through the Slacker Radio Service

+ Listening to Podcasts

+ Watching Videos

+ BlackBerry PlayBook Video Chat

The BlackBerry PlayBook is not just a big-screen BlackBerry smartphone, and that becomes obvious when you start using it to enjoy multimedia on the 7-inch display with rocking stereo speakers. You can enjoy your own music collection; browse and purchase music from 7digital; stream music from Slacker; subscribe, download, and listen to podcasts; capture and watch your own videos; stream videos; and even communicate with friends via Video Chat. You can enjoy these forms of media directly on the PlayBook or output to your TV via the HDMI connection.

Enjoying Music Loaded onto Your PlayBook

The BlackBerry PlayBook comes preloaded with a Music application that you can use to enjoy music (see Figure 9-1). The music player is integrated into the OS so that you can even control your music from the Status bar, detailed in Chapter 3 (How Do I Navigate My PlayBook?), while you use other applications at the same time. The PlayBook is a multitasking workhorse, and music shows this off better than anything, with flawless playback as other applications run in the foreground.

FIGURE 9-1 Main Music application Home screen

You can listen to music in the following audio formats:

+ MP3
+ AAC
+ M4A
+ WMA
+ WAV

The most common formats used by desktop clients are MP3 and AAC, so you should not have any problems playing your non-DRM music on your PlayBook.

TRANSFERRING MUSIC TO YOUR PLAYBOOK

You can transfer your existing music collection to your PlayBook in a couple of ways:

+ Connect to a Windows or Mac computer and transfer music via USB or Wi-Fi.
+ Connect to a Windows computer and use the BlackBerry Desktop Software (discussed in detail in Chapter 15, [How Do I Manage My PlayBook with BlackBerry Desktop Software?]) to manage your media transfers.

Transferring Music via USB or Wi-Fi

When you connect your PlayBook to a Windows or Mac computer using either USB or Wi-Fi, the internal storage (16GB, 32GB, or 64GB) appears as another drive on your computer. Figure 9-2 shows how it appears on a Windows PC.

HOW DO I CONNECT MY PLAYBOOK TO MY MAC OR PC VIA WI-FI?
Since most mp3 players and video cameras use USB to transfer music between device and computer, USB transfer will likely be the most popular method to perform the tasks discussed in this chapter. See Chapter 10, (How Can I View, Share, and Capture Pictures on My PlayBook?) to learn step-by-step how to transfer files (pictures, video, and music) from a computer to your PlayBook wirelessly.

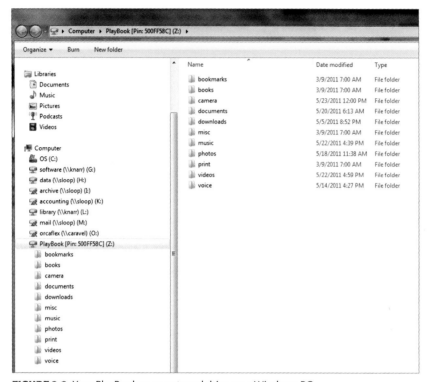

FIGURE 9-2 Your PlayBook as an external drive on a Windows PC

Following are the steps to get music onto your device after you connect using the USB cable or via Wi-Fi to your Windows or Mac computer.

1. Connect your PlayBook via USB cable or Wi-Fi to your computer.

2. Find music stored on your computer, and then drag and drop or copy and paste it into the Music folder on your PlayBook storage drive.

3. Your music then appears on your PlayBook with filters for All, Artists, Albums, and Genres. All of your music exists in the All folder, but can be sorted using these filters. Playlists are not supported using this external drive transfer method, as discussed later in the chapter.

Transferring Music via BlackBerry Desktop Software

To transfer music via BlackBerry Desktop software, you need a Windows computer and a USB cable. Use the Media Sync feature to sync your Music content from Windows Media Player or iTunes with your PlayBook after connecting via USB or Bluetooth. See Chapter 15 (How Do I Manage My PlayBook with BlackBerry Desktop Software?) for step-by-step instructions on the details and functionality of the desktop software.

CAN I TRANSFER MUSIC FROM MY MAC TO MY PLAYBOOK USING BLACKBERRY DESKTOP SOFTWARE? As of this writing, BlackBerry Desktop Software is not yet available for Apple Mac computers, but RIM stated in May of 2011 that it is currently under development.

CREATING PLAYLISTS AND ORGANIZING YOUR MUSIC

The BlackBerry PlayBook Music utility is a streamlined application with basic functionality in a few areas, including playlists and music organization by category. You can see a default playlist in the Music application after you launch it, labeled PlayBook Playlist. To add songs to this playlist, follow these steps:

1. From within the Music application, swipe your finger down from the top frame of the display to open the menu.

2. Tap the Edit button (Pencil icon on far right), as shown in Figure 9-3. A small pop-up appears instructing you to select the songs you want to add to this playlist.

FIGURE 9-3 Edit button in the upper menu

3. Tap songs you want to put into the playlist. Note that tapping on songs makes a selection with a check mark to the far right of the song list.

4. After making your song selections, tap the Add button to add the songs to your PlayBook Playlist.

You can also remove songs from this playlist by following these steps:

1. Follow steps 1-2 in the previous list describing how to add songs.

2. Tap the Edit button (Pencil icon on far right). A small pop-up appears instructing you to select the songs you want to remove from this playlist.

3. Tap on songs you want to remove from the playlist. Note that tapping on songs makes a selection with a check mark to the far right of the song list. When removing songs from the PlayBook playlist, you also have a new button to Select All (see Figure 9-4). Tap this to select all the songs in the playlist.

4. After making your song selections, tap the Remove button to remove the songs from your PlayBook Playlist.

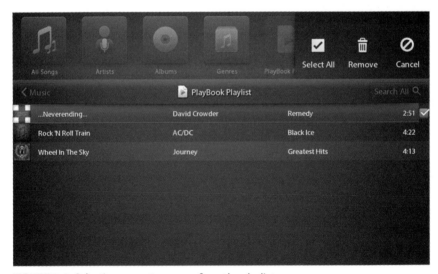

FIGURE 9-4 Selecting songs to remove from the playlist

Other than the default PlayBook Playlist, RIM does not support playlist
creation or removal on the PlayBook. Therefore, the only way to create a new
playlist is on your PC; then select to sync that playlist to your PlayBook via the
Media Sync feature. If you do sync a playlist from your PC to your PlayBook,
such as the Classic Rock one shown in Figure 9-5, you can select songs from
within it to add to the default PlayBook playlist following the same steps for
adding songs to a playlist, but you cannot add or remove songs from this
synced playlist.

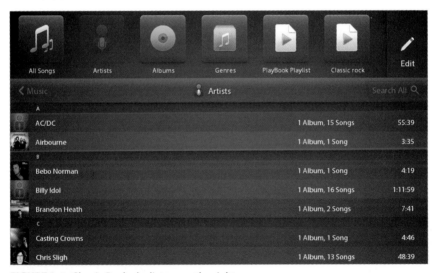

FIGURE 9-5 Classic Rock playlist up on the right

PLAYING AND CONTROLLING MUSIC

You can control how and when your music plays on the PlayBook using either
the controllers on the upper Status bar within the Music application or via the

hardware buttons on top of the PlayBook. To start playing music within the Music application, you can perform one of the following:

✦ Tap a song in the All Songs list to play a single song.

✦ Tap an album's art to play all songs in a selected album.

✦ Tap an album in a list from a particular artist to play all albums from that particular artist.

✦ Tap a song in a genre list to play all songs in that genre.

The in-app music controller appears at the bottom of the display, as shown in Figure 9-6. From left to right, these are the controls available to you:

✦ **Back**: This button takes you back to the beginning of a song with one tap, and tapping again takes you back to the previous song in your current play session.

✦ **Play/Pause**: Use this button to play the song or pause it, and the button changes to the opposite function after one action is carried out.

✦ **Stop**: Press this button to stop the song playing and hide the bottom music controller interface.

✦ **Forward**: This button moves to the next song in your play session.

FIGURE 9-6 Music controls at the bottom of the display

+ **Album art history**: If you tap the small arrow to the right of the Forward button, the player controls slide up to reveal a graphical user interface that enables you to jump to other songs in the particular play session by tapping and sliding album art right and left.

+ **Album Art**: The icon to the right of the cover flow toggle is the album art.

+ **Song slider**: The song and album name appear on a wide bar and as the song plays the bar moves to the right to display the progression of the song. Tap anywhere on the slider or slide your finger along it to control your place within the song. At the right end of the slider bar, you can see the elapsed time and total time for the song.

+ **Shuffle and Repeat**: The small Repeat button is on top of the Shuffle button. Tap either of these toggles on the respective feature to either continuously play the selected song or shuffle between songs in the album, artist, genre, or all songs session you initiated.

+ **Volume slider**: Control the volume using either of the hardware buttons or the on-screen slider bar found at the far right of the music controller.

HARDWARE BUTTONS FUNCTION AS A MUSIC CONTROLLER There are engraved symbols on the volume buttons to indicate their functionality. The volume up button also serves as a Back button and volume down doubles as a Forward button when you press and hold them down for a couple of seconds. The center button serves as a Play/Pause button when media is playing.

If you minimize the Music application, you can see a Media Player icon in the top Status bar, shown as a blue arrow. Tap once on it to see a pop-up appear, as shown in Figure 9-7, with the following controls and features:

+ Album art
+ Elapsed and total time
+ Artist name

+ Song name
+ Back button
+ Play/Pause button
+ Forward button

Tap the Media Player icon again to hide this pop-up and continue to play your music.

FIGURE 9-7 Pop-up music controller

Browsing and Purchasing Music through the 7digital Music Store

One of the reasons Apple's iPod and iPhone devices are popular is because the ecosystem in which they thrive provides media with little effort required from the consumer. Similar to Apple's iTunes, RIM includes the 7digital Music Store service and application on the PlayBook so that you can browse, preview, purchase, and download songs right from your PlayBook tablet from its collection of more than 13 million songs. 7digital provides high-quality, non-DRM MP3 files at 320kbps, so you can purchase and download from your PlayBook, and then play the same songs on your BlackBerry smartphone, desktop computer, or other media player. 7digital also has an integrated recommendation engine, so it can "learn" what you enjoy listening to, and then help you find what you like in its extensive catalog of titles. It has album specials as low as $5 and offers competitive pricing for music.

To access the 7digital Music Store and discover music to purchase on your PlayBook follow these steps:

1. Under the All or Media tab, tap the Music Store icon.

2. Use the tabs at the top of the display to filter music through the following categories:

   ✦ Featured

   ✦ New Releases

   ✦ Best Sellers

   ✦ Genres

3. After you find something that interests you, tap the album art to see
   the album price and per song price (see Figure 9-8).

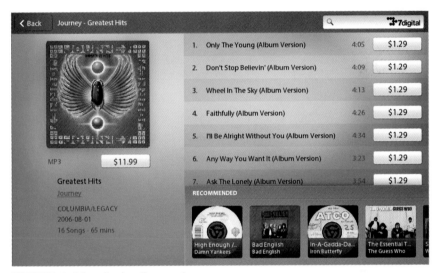

FIGURE 9-8 Prices for the album and songs

4. Tap a song name on the right side of your display to play a preview,
   ranging from 30 seconds to 1 minute.

5. If you want to purchase the song, tap the price in the far right side of
   the song selection. A confirmation pop-up appears; then tap Buy Now
   to make the purchase, as shown in Figure 9-9.

6. If this is your first purchase, fill out the credit card information as 7digi-
   tal prompts you.

7. The song then downloads and appears with a Play button instead of a
   Price button in the song list. It also appears in your My Purchases tab
   and on your PlayBook's internal storage.

FIGURE 9-9 Purchase pop-up

SEE THE RECOMMENDED ALBUMS AT THE BOTTOM? As you browse music and make purchases, 7digital provides album recommendations in the bottom-right corner as you look through its catalog offerings.

Listening to Music through the Slacker Radio Service

Slacker Radio is a streaming-only online radio service that comes as a pre-loaded shortcut on your PlayBook and only requires an active data connection and free account to function. Slacker Radio is set up with channels based on genre, so you can select a genre and then hear what it provides in the random playlist. You can view reviews, lyrics, and artist biographies. Slacker Radio also "learns" what you like and dislike if you actively tap the heart icon if you like a song and crossed out circle icon if you dislike a song. Slacker Radio then attempts to create a dynamic playlist that matches your favorites. You can see album art for the song that is playing and also see what is coming next, with the ability to skip upcoming songs (limited to six skips with the free service and unlimited with a subscription).

SIGN UP FOR A FREE ACCOUNT When you first launch Slacker Radio you are prompted to sign in to an existing account or sign up for a new one. Enter your email, password (twice), year of birth, gender, and postal code to sign up for a free account right from your PlayBook.

Now take a look at the user interface of Slacker Radio on your PlayBook, as shown in Figure 9-10.

FIGURE 9-10 Slacker Radio user interface

✛ **Top bar on the display**: The station currently playing appears in the far left of the upper bar, and on the far right is a Quick Search box where you can search Slacker for an artist, song, album, or station. The Gear icon is for your settings, and tapping it shows your account details with the option to reset your account and log back in to use the service.

SEARCH BOX FOR QUICK ACCESS Use the search box to find some-thing you want immediately. After entering a search term, you see a Play button you can push to jump to that artist, song, or album, as shown in Figure 9-11. Slacker Radio auto-filters as you type text in the box to help you find things faster.

FIGURE 9-11 Searching in Slacker Radio

+ **Upper one-third of the display**: Shows the album art of the playing song with the song name, artist name, album name, and a timeline with elapsed and total time. There are also buttons for Play/Pause, Skip, Like, and Dislike. The album art for the next song appears on the far right and the previously played album art appears to the left (refer to Figure 9-10).

+ **Bar under the upper one-third**: Here you can find buttons for Artist bio (see Figure 9-12) Album review, and Lyrics. Tap Home to return to the Slacker Radio Home screen:

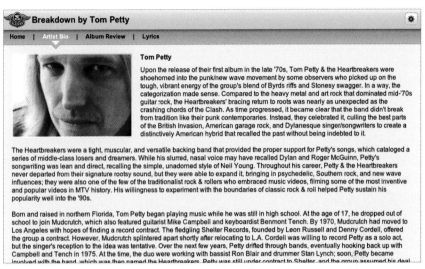

FIGURE 9-12 You can choose to view the artist bio, album information, and lyrics.

- **Left hand column**: You can browse the various Slacker Radio categories, including:
  - Favorites
  - Recently played
  - My stations
  - Top stations
  - Various genres
- **Right-side column (takes most of the display)**: This is the station control area. Tap the far right Play icon for the particular station you want to listen to after filtering through a category/genre in the left column.

You cannot select stations as favorites with the Slacker Radio application on the PlayBook and must manage stations from your web browser. The Slacker Radio application is used to play the music you set up through your online account.

AMAZON CLOUD PLAYER WORKS TOO The web browser on the PlayBook is powerful enough to support several different streaming music services in addition to or in lieu of Slacker Radio. For instance, you can use the Amazon Cloud Player service to stream music to your PlayBook. You can upload your own music collection or purchase music from Amazon's MP3 store and enjoy it on your PlayBook with an active data connection.

Listening to Podcasts

Podcasts are audio and video broadcasts recorded by people who want to share their work with others. I co-host the MobileTechRoundup (MoTR) podcast and listen to podcasts for hours on my commute. Thus, I was pleased to discover that RIM includes an application for podcasts, aptly named Podcasts. After launching the Podcasts application, you can first see the Featured tab, as shown Figure 9-13. You can then jump to the Categories, Downloads, or My Podcasts page to discover and view different podcasts.

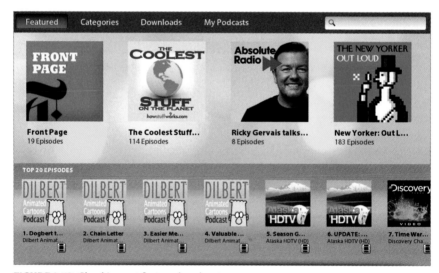

FIGURE 9-13 Checking out featured podcasts

SUBSCRIBE TO PODCASTS

When you subscribe to a podcast, you designate the show as one you want to download and receive updates from when future shows are released. The first step to subscribing is to find a podcast you want to listen to or view. You can use the Featured or Categories tab to discover podcasts by tapping around on the various icons. On the Featured tab you can perform the following steps to get shows on your PlayBook:

1. Swipe your finger right and left to view what podcasts are featured for that day.

2. Tap on the Podcast icon for a show that interests you. It then opens up to the podcast page with details on the show and a listing on the right of recorded shows you can download (see Figure 9-14).

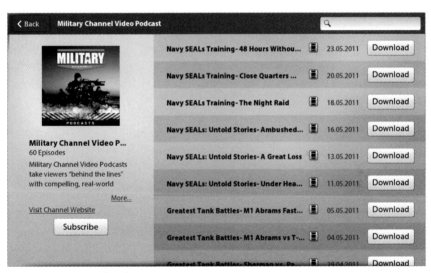

FIGURE 9-14 Typical podcast page

3. Tap the Download button to download the show episode to your PlayBook. By choosing to download an episode, you are also choosing to subscribe to that podcast. If you want to subscribe to the show without downloading anything at the time, tap the Subscribe button below the show description.

You can also find podcasts by tapping the Categories tab and browsing through all the different categories included in the Podcasts application (see Figure 9-15). To see all the podcasts you are subscribed to, tap the My Podcasts tab to view subscribed channels or downloaded episodes.

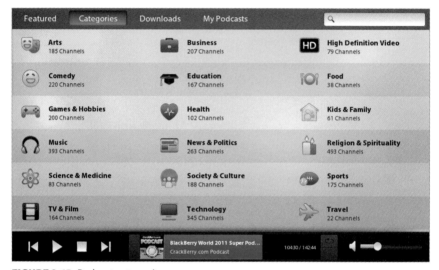

FIGURE 9-15 Podcast categories

I DON'T SEE MY FAVORITE PODCAST As of this writing there is no capability to subscribe to podcasts that are not already in the catalog of offerings within the Podcasts application.

DOWNLOAD AND ENJOY PODCASTS

After subscribing to shows that interest you, visit the podcast options' settings to control when and how many episodes download to your PlayBook. To access and control these options:

1. Swipe down from the top frame.

2. Tap the Options button, and the podcast options page appears (see Figure 9-16).

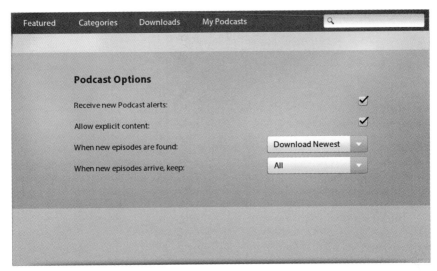

FIGURE 9-16 Podcast options

To view the episodes you download, follow these steps:

1. Tap on the Downloads tab, as shown in Figure 9-17. Here you see the show and a Play button.

2. Tap the Play button to start the podcast, and you see a player controller, just like the one detailed earlier for the Music application, appear on the bottom of your display. Episodes with video have a slightly different player, as shown in Figure 9-18.

3. Use the controls to pause, play, fast-forward, and rewind your episode. When you finish, you can tap the X button on the Downloads tab next to a podcast to delete that episode from your PlayBook.

PODCASTS CAN BE CONTROLLED FROM THE STATUS BAR Just like the Music application, you can control podcast playback using the media player hardware buttons on the top of the PlayBook or by using the upper Status bar player controller.

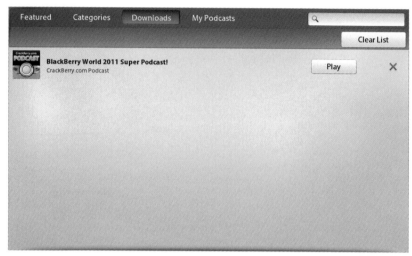

FIGURE 9-17 Downloads tab

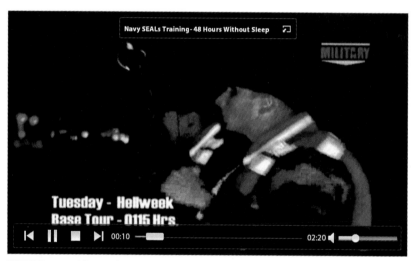

FIGURE 9-18 Video podcast controls

Watching Videos

Unlike with music and podcasts, there is currently no specific ecosystem for video content on the PlayBook. You can, however, view videos you recorded on your PlayBook with other devices such as a computer, smartphone, or camera, with an HDMI connection. Supported video formats include H.264 and MPEG-4.

TRANSFERRING VIDEOS ONTO YOUR PLAYBOOK

Similar to the methods you learned in the Transferring Music To Your PlayBook section, you can connect your PlayBook to your PC or Mac and use the external drive mode to drag and drop videos into the Videos folder on your storage drive or use BlackBerry Desktop Software to manage video transfer. See Chapter 15 for more details on managing your video content via BlackBerry Desktop Software.

RECORDING VIDEOS WITH YOUR PLAYBOOK

Your PlayBook also has capable front- and rear-facing cameras, so you can record videos right from your device. To record a video, follow these steps:

1. Tap the Camera application from either the Home screen or Media tab and then either toggle to video capture or swipe down from the top frame in the Videos application and tap on the Take Videos icon in the upper left (see Figure 9-19).

2. Tap the red Record button to start capturing video. Tap it again to stop recording. There is no pause capability, so each time you press stop another video file is created.

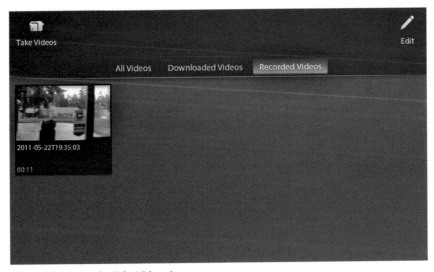

FIGURE 9-19 Tap the Take Videos icon

When recording video on your PlayBook, you can perform a couple of options:

+ Tap the display, and tap the Switch icon in the lower right to switch from the default rear-facing camera to the front-facing camera to capture video of yourself.

+ Swipe down from the top frame to access the following video camera settings:

    + **Video capture resolution**: Choose from 480p, 720p HD, or 1080p HD quality (see Figure 9-20).

    + **Video mode**: Auto, sports, or whiteboard options are available, just like when taking still camera shots as detailed in Chapter 10 (How Can I View, Share, and Capture Pictures on my PlayBook?).

FIGURE 9-20 Video capture resolution options

- -

HOW MUCH STORAGE DOES VIDEO CONSUME? Video recorded at 1080p resolution consumes about 120MB for each minute of recording, whereas video recorded at 480p consumes about 20MB for each minute.

- -

You can choose to delete videos directly from your PlayBook by taking these steps:

1. Swipe down from the top frame.

2. Tap the Edit button.

3. Tap each video you want to delete.

4. Tap the Delete button (Trash Can icon) and confirm by tapping Delete on the pop-up, as shown in Figure 9-21.

FIGURE 9-21 Selecting videos to delete

PLAYING AND CONTROLLING VIDEOS

You can enjoy videos on your PlayBook or output them via HDMI to a large display or TV. The video player has controls similar to the music player, including support for the hardware player buttons and upper Status bar player controls.

Watching Videos Directly on Your PlayBook

To watch videos directly on your PlayBook display, first browse through your video collection and decide what video you want to play; then follow these steps:

1. Tap the video thumbnail, and the video immediately opens up in a full page and starts playing.

2. Tap the display to access the video controls, as shown in Figure 9-22, that include the following:

+ **Back**: Takes you to the previous video in your collection

+ **Play/Pause**: Starts playback or pauses playback

+ **Forward**: Jumps to the next video in your collection

+ **Video timeline**: Enables you to see where you are in the video file while also enabling you to tap and slide to where you want to go within the video

+ **Repeat button**: Loops your video continuously

+ **Volume controller**: Control the volume levels

FIGURE 9-22 Video player controls

You can also control video playback using the controls from the upper Status bar as you did with music. This control does not appear to be as useful for video though because tapping Play here starts the video in the minimized window, so you can hear the audio but only see the video in a small window (see Figure 9-23).

FIGURE 9-23 Video player controls

Watching Videos via HDMI

Videos are more enjoyable when played on a display or a compatible big screen HD television using an HDMI cable; you can output those great videos you capture of the kids to share with grandma during a visit. To play your videos on a big screen, simply connect your HDMI cable to the ports on your TV and PlayBook, and operate the video player just like you would if you were watching them on your PlayBook.

WATCHING YOUTUBE VIDEOS

RIM included a YouTube application on the PlayBook that you can use to watch YouTube videos. To do so, follow these steps:

1. Tap the YouTube application from the Home screen.

2. Find a video to watch, and use the YouTube player control buttons to view the video on your PlayBook, as shown in Figure 9-24.

3. Tap the button in the lower-right corner of the video to maximize to full screen mode; the video controllers now appear on the display when you tap it once (see Figure 9-25). These controls include play, pause, timeline, and volume controls.

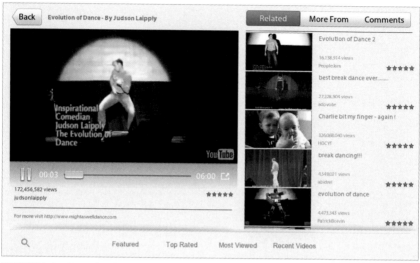

FIGURE 9-24 YouTube player controls

FIGURE 9-25 Full screen mode and controls

YouTube video browsing is provided in the following categories and also contains a search feature:

- Featured
- Top rated
- Most viewed
- Recent videos

Unlike some other mobile YouTube applications, you cannot sign into your YouTube account and view your videos or rent any from YouTube on the PlayBook using this application.

BlackBerry PlayBook Video Chat

Video Chat on the PlayBook is one of the highest quality video chat experiences on a mobile device, in large part because the exchange is handled through RIM's servers, so it is optimized for the PlayBook experience. The service supports video chatting between PlayBook owners on Wi-Fi connections only and is not compatible with desktop computers, so you need to find friends with PlayBooks to carry out a conversation.

INITIATE A VIDEO CHAT SESSION

Once you find someone to chat with, perform the following steps to initiate a conversation:

1. Tap the New Contact from the main Video Chat display, and a new video chat contact card appears, as shown in Figure 9-26.

FIGURE 9-26 Adding a new contact

2. Enter your friend's BlackBerry ID username and a display name you want your friend to appear as on your PlayBook.

3. Tap the Video Chat icon to the right of the BlackBerry ID field to initiate a call.

If you already have an existing list of contacts, simply tap your contact's image or name to initiate a call. Your contacts appear in tabbed categories for all contacts, recent contacts, and frequent contacts to help you find the person quickly. You can also remove contacts from your list by swiping down on the upper frame and selecting contacts to remove.

- -

VOICE-ONLY CALLS ARE POSSIBLE, TOO By default, calls initiated within the Video Chat application are video calls. However, if you are on a bandwidth restricted Wi-Fi network or are having a bad hair day, you can tap the toggle in the upper left (see Figure 9-27) and switch to audio-only calls.

FIGURE 9-27 Toggle audio and video

- -

CONTROL IN-CALL FUNCTIONS

By default, the Video Chat application provides a full screen experience with no buttons or controls visible to either caller. Your friend appears on most of the display with a small box in the right corner displaying the picture of you that your friend sees. Figure 9-28 shows a video chat between me and a friend, Kevin Tofel from GigaOm.

FIGURE 9-28 Video Chat in session

YOU CAN MOVE YOURSELF Although your video image appears in the upper right by default, you can touch and drag your preview image to a different corner, as you prefer.

Tap once on the display to bring up a bottom control bar with the following options, as shown in Figure 9-29:

- **Camera Switch**: Tap this button to toggle between the front-facing camera (on by default for these calls) and rear-facing camera. You can use the rear-facing camera to show your friend what is going on around you, (also a great way to share the grandkids with grandma).

+ **End Call**: A red Phone icon appears in the center of the display that you can tap to end the call.

+ **Mute**: Tap this button to mute audio on your side of the call. Tap it again to turn the microphone back on.

+ **Volume**: You can control incoming volume levels using this slider bar.

FIGURE 9-29 Video player controls

MANAGE CALL NOTIFICATIONS

Your friends may also call you, and you can choose to accept or reject the call when the pop-up appears. You also have the ability to accept the call as voice-only, in case you don't feel like showing off your face to your friend.

You can view and manage your chat history by following these steps:

1. Tap the Recent tab from the main Video Chat display page to see a history of your chat sessions, as shown on Figure 9-30.

2. Swipe down from the upper frame to pull up a menu of editing options, including Clear List, Edit, and Help.

3. Tap edit, and then tap the Trash Can icon next to each chat history you want to remove. You can also clear the list to delete all your history.

FIGURE 9-30 Recent history

WHAT'S THE CAMERA IN THE UPPER RIGHT FOR? If you tap the Camera icon in the upper right of your screen, it shows you a video preview of what your friend can expect to see. This shows only a preview for the front-facing camera and not what will be seen from the rear-facing camera.

Video Chat does not need to be running on your PlayBook for you to get call requests from your friends. Therefore in the upper-left corner there is an icon three in from the left for Do Not Disturb, as shown in Figure 9-31. If you enable this, then you cannot receive any notifications of incoming video chat requests, but they will still be recorded in your chat history. The caller receives a message that you are unavailable. If you do turn this on, don't forget to turn it off if you ever want to receive incoming calls again.

FIGURE 9-31 Toggle on Do Not Disturb

Related Questions

➕ Where can I find media apps? **PAGE 198**

➕ Where else can I control my media settings? **PAGES 268 AND 274**

➕ How can I use the BlackBerry Desktop software to sync media to my PlayBook? **PAGE 283**

HOW CAN I VIEW, SHARE, AND CAPTURE PICTURES ON MY PLAYBOOK?

In this chapter:

+ Transferring Photos on and off Your PlayBook
+ Capturing a Photo
+ Viewing Your Pictures
+ Sharing Your Pictures

The 7-inch display on the BlackBerry PlayBook is perfect for viewing photos, especially when set on the desktop stand where it can function as a digital photo frame. You can transfer photos to your PlayBook and then share them with friends and family on the device or on a large HD television or monitor. RIM also includes a couple of high-resolution cameras, so you can capture photos on-the-go that look great.

Transferring Photos on and off Your PlayBook

As Chapter 9 (How Do I Enjoy Music and Video on My PlayBook?) describes, there are several ways to transfer files onto your PlayBook. The following methods are supported for transferring photos onto your BlackBerry PlayBook:

✦ Transfer photos via USB cable between your PlayBook and your PC or Mac.

✦ Transfer photos wirelessly between your PlayBook and your PC or Mac.

✦ Transfer photos via BlackBerry Desktop Software with your PC or Mac. This process is explained in detail in Chapter 15 (How Do I Manage My PlayBook with BlackBerry Desktop Software?).

Several other ways exist to transfer photos, but most are not supported. The following are some popular ways to transfer photos that your BlackBerry PlayBook does not support:

✦ Transferring content directly from a camera memory card is not supported because your PlayBook does not have an external storage slot or a USB host support capable of transferring files onto the device.

✦ Transferring photos wirelessly from a Bluetooth-enabled smartphone is not supported because RIM only supports four Bluetooth profiles on the PlayBook, none of which include support for Bluetooth file transfer.

✦ Transferring photos from BlackBerry Bridge connected to BlackBerry smartphones is also not currently supported.

USB PHOTO SHARING ON A WINDOWS 7 PC

To connect your PlayBook to your Windows 7 PC for file sharing via USB, follow these steps:

1. Connect the microUSB cable to your PlayBook and computer.

2. If this is the first time you have made the connection, perform the following instructions in this step; if you already have BlackBerry Device Manager installed, skip to step 3.

   A. A pop-up appears in the lower-right corner stating that drivers are being installed, followed by a large pop-up, as shown in Figure 10-1, with a CD Drive labeled: BlackBerry PlayBook .

   B. Click Run setup.exe to run the setup program. An InstallShield Wizard starts so that you can install BlackBerry Device Manager software.

   FIGURE 10-1 Device Manager installation prompt

   C. Follow the prompts in the wizard, primarily clicking the Next button, to set up the software for your PlayBook. This includes accepting the EULA and the final Install button.

   D. After clicking the Finish button, disconnect and reconnect your PlayBook (see Figure 10-2).

   FIGURE 10-2 Disconnect after driver installation.

3. You then see a pop-up in the lower-right corner stating that BlackBerry Device Manager has recognized your PlayBook [Pin: 500AAAAA] mass storage and assigned it a drive letter. The Pin is specific to your PlayBook and the characters will change depending on what Pin your device has

assigned to it. You can also notice that the display on your PlayBook shows that you are connected to a computer, as shown in Figure 10-3.

FIGURE 10-3 PlayBook status message

4. Open File Explorer, click your PlayBook drive, and then you see default directories for the following, as shown in Figure 10-4:

+ Bookmarks

+ Books

+ Camera

+ Documents

+ Downloads

+ Misc

+ Music

+ Photos

+ Print

+ Videos

+ Voice

5. You can then transfer photos to and from the Photos directory just like you can with any other File Explorer file transfers.

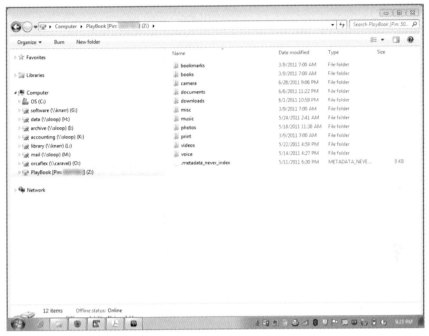

FIGURE 10-4 File Explorer view of your PlayBook

LIMITS ON PLACING PHOTOS If you try to place photos in the root directory of your PlayBook, you see a security warning, as shown in Figure 10-5. Make sure to place your photos in the Photos directory to ensure that the PlayBook properly recognizes them when you disconnect from the USB cable.

FIGURE 10-5 Security warning during transfer attempt

USB PHOTO SHARING ON A MAC

To connect your PlayBook to your Apple Mac for file sharing via USB, follow these steps:

1. Connect the microUSB cable to your PlayBook and computer.

2. If this is the first time you have made the connection, follow these steps; if you already have BlackBerry Device Manager installed, skip to step 3.

   A. On the desktop or within Finder, double-click BlackBerry PlayBookCD.

   B. Double-click the BlackBerry Device Manager Installer to start the installation process.

   C. Follow the prompts in the wizard, primarily clicking the Next button, to set up the software for your PlayBook. This includes accepting the EULA and the final Install button.

   D. After clicking the Finish button, reboot your Mac. After the reboot is complete and the PlayBook is connected again, a message may appear stating that a new network interface has been detected. If this is the case, click Open Network Preferences, as shown in Figure 10-6.

   E. You should then see your PlayBook show up as a RIM Network Device within the Network Preferences. Click Apply to accept the connection.

FIGURE 10-6 Network setup prompt on a Mac

3. Your PlayBook shows up as a network drive on your desktop with the PlayBook (500AAAAA) label and under the Shared area of your Finder,

as shown in Figure 10-7. The Pin is specific to your PlayBook and the characters change depending on what Pin your device assigns it.

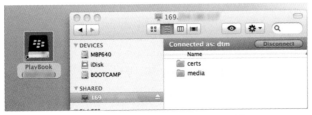

FIGURE 10-7 PlayBook appears in two areas on a Mac.

4. Click your PlayBook drive from the desktop, and you see the following folders:

✦ Bookmarks

✦ Books

✦ Camera

✦ Documents

✦ Downloads

✦ Misc

✦ Music

✦ Photos

✦ Print

✦ Videos

✦ Voice

If you click your PlayBook in the Shared area of your Finder, you see a directory for certs as well. Certs is the folder where you store security certificates you wish to install and use on your PlayBook.

5. You can then transfer photos to and from the Photos directory just like you can with any other Finder file transfers.

WI-FI PHOTO SHARING

RIM made it easy for you to get photos and files on and off the PlayBook thanks to its advanced support for Wi-Fi file sharing. This capability works for both Windows and Mac computers. First, you need to enable Wi-Fi file sharing from your PlayBook by following these steps:

1. Tap the Settings icon in the far top-right corner on your PlayBook. The Settings area opens up.

2. Tap the Storage and Sharing setting in the left list of available settings.

3. Swipe your finger from the bottom up to scroll down to the bottom of this settings page where the Wi-Fi Sharing option is found. Slide the toggle to ON, as shown in Figure 10-8.

4. Slide the toggle to ON for Password Protect also because you are required to have a password to share media on a PlayBook. A pop-up appears for you to enter a password and confirm it, so enter the password of your choice twice and tap the OK button.

FIGURE 10-8 Wi-Fi Sharing toggle

CHECK YOUR USERNAME If you want to share media files on your PlayBook, you need to know some key information. In the Storage & Sharing settings area, you can find the properties of your PlayBook in the Network Identification area. Make sure you note what the username of your PlayBook is before leaving this area.

5. To connect your PlayBook to your computer, you need the IP address of your PlayBook. To find out what this is, tap the About option (in your left menu) in Settings and tap the drop-down in the view information line. Select the Network option and make a note of the IPv4 address of your PlayBook, as shown in Figure 10-9. You need to enter this into your computer later, so you may want to write it down or memorize it.

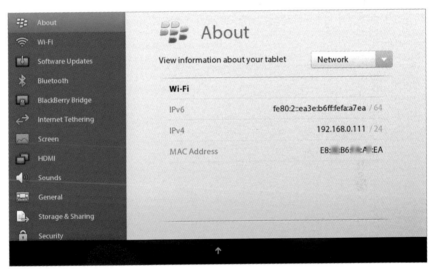

FIGURE 10-9 Note the IP address of your PlayBook.

6. Choose the next set of steps to follow depending on the type of computer you use to access your PlayBook:

Windows computer:

A. On your Windows computer, select Start ⇨ Run, and a pop-up appears. Alternatively, if you do not have a Run option, just begin step 2 by typing in the search box.

B. On the Open line, enter the IP address of your PlayBook in the format \\192.168.0.155 where the numbers are replaced by your specific IP address (see Figure 10-10). Click the OK button.

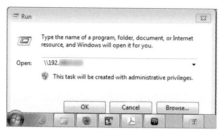

FIGURE 10-10 Enter your IP address.

C. Your File Explorer opens with volume selections for certs and media.

D. Double-click the media volume, and a pop-up appears, as shown in Figure 10-11.

FIGURE 10-11 Enter your PlayBook username and password.

E. Enter your PlayBook username and password; then click OK. The media drive folders appear just like the ones detailed in the USB connection section.

F. You can then transfer photos to and from the Photos and Camera directories just like you can with any other File Explorer file transfers.

Mac computer:

A. On your Mac, select Go ⇨ Connect to Server.

B. Enter the IP address of your PlayBook in the format smb://192.168.0.555 where the numbers are replaced by your specific IP address.

C. Click the Connect button, and a dialog box appears (see Figure 10-12). With the registered user option selected, enter the username you noted in the Network Identification area and the password you entered in step 3.

FIGURE 10-12 Setting up the connection on a Mac

D. Click Connect. A pop-up appears with volume selection for certs and media.

E. Select the media volume and click the OK button. Your PlayBook directories appear in the Shared network area of your Finder just like when you connected via the USB cable.

F. You can then transfer photos to and from the Photos and Camera directories just like you can with any other Finder file transfers.

CHECK TO REMEMBER PASSWORD If you connect your PlayBook with the same computers on a regular basis and are comfortable with your computer's security settings, you may want to click the options to remember your password and credentials when connecting via Wi-Fi so that you won't have to do it every time.

You can eject the network connection on your Mac and turn off Wi-Fi shar-ing or the Wi-Fi radio on your PlayBook to close down the network connection when you finish transferring files.

Capturing a Photo

Your PlayBook has a 5-megapixel rear-facing camera and a 3-megapixel front-facing camera with the capability to capture digital photos and video in 1080p HD resolution. Video capture is covered in Chapter 9 (How Do I Enjoy Music and Video on My PlayBook?) The camera controls are basic and easy to use; the optics and camera module capture clear photos you can share with family and friends. To capture a picture with the rear facing 5-megapixel camera, fol-low these steps:

1. Tap the Camera application icon to launch the camera. There is no cap-ture hardware button to start the camera.

2. Aim your PlayBook at your subject, and tap the large Camera button (shutter release) located on the right (in landscape) or bottom (in por-trait) of your display, as shown Figure 10-13.

FIGURE 10-13 Capture a photo by tapping the Camera button.

Although taking a photo is that simple, you may also want to have a bit more control over your photos and the way they are captured. The two previous steps are what you use for a fully automatic quick-start photo shoot. If you launch the Camera application and then tap on the display outside of the camera Capture button, you can see a few more options appear, as follows (orientation assumes landscape mode) as shown in Figure 10-14:

+ **Upper left**: This display shows the selected camera mode; A for auto shows by default. The other modes are Sports and Whiteboard, detailed later in this chapter.

+ **Left side**: Zoom in and out by sliding your finger up and down the zoom slider bar. The PlayBook has a 2.5x digital zoom with no optical zoom support.

+ **Bottom left**: Toggle the geo-location function on and off using this button.

+ **Bottom right**: Toggle between front and rear-facing cameras.

FIGURE 10-14 On-screen camera control options

The Camera application also has an upper menu. Simply slide your finger from the upper frame down to the display to reveal the following menu options, working from the far left to the right, as shown in Figure 10-15:

+ **Pictures**: Tap the photo viewer, which the following section describes.

✦ **Stabilization**: This button toggles image stabilization on and off, and by default it is off. Enabling this should help reduce image blurriness if you have trouble holding the PlayBook still while tapping the Shutter Release button.

✦ **Ratio**: You can toggle between 4:3 and 16:9 aspect ratios. The 16:9 ratio is the default and likely to be used most of the time. 4:3 captures images at 2592x1944 (5 megapixel) resolution, whereas 16:9 captures images at 2592x1456 (3.7 megapixel) resolution.

✦ **Auto, Sports, and Whiteboard**: By default, the Auto mode is selected. Sport mode is intended to help capture faster action, and Whiteboard is designed to help in properly contrasting and focusing on words against a bright backdrop.

FIGURE 10-15 Camera menu options

You can toggle to the front-facing camera to capture photos of yourself or others looking at the PlayBook display, as shown in Figure 10-16. All the same options and functions in the rear-facing camera are available to you when using the front-facing camera. The resolution changes mean that photos captured with the front-facing camera in 4:3 ratio are 2048x1536 (3 megapixel) and with 16:9 ratio the photos have 2048x1152 (2.35 megapixel) resolution.

FIGURE 10-16 Photo captured with front-facing camera

There is no flash on the PlayBook, so to get the best photo quality, you need to make sure you have ample lighting available. Photos captured outdoors generally tend to be best on the PlayBook.

Viewing Your Pictures

In the Pictures application you can view all pictures captured, downloaded, or transferred to your PlayBook. Pinch-to-zoom gestures are supported, and it is quick and easy to browse through your photos. To view your pictures, start by launching the Pictures application, and you see albums appear on your display, as shown in Figure 10-17. Similar to playlists, albums cannot be created on your PlayBook. RIM does provide you with four default albums into which all your photos are automatically categorized. These four albums are:

+ All pictures
+ Camera pictures
+ Downloads
+ Wallpaper

FIGURE 10-17 Default Pictures application Home screen

Once a default album has photos in it, up to four thumbnails appear on your display for each album. If you really want more albums than just those four, you can create folders on your connected PC or Mac, load them up with photos, and then when you view them on the PlayBook, they become your albums. Figure 10-18 shows a Hawaii 2011 album on my PlayBook that I created by dragging a folder of Hawaii photos from my PC to my PlayBook when connected via USB.

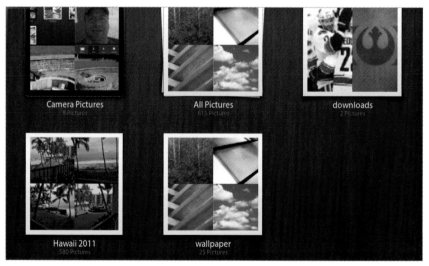

FIGURE 10-18 Folder from a PC becomes an album in Pictures.

WHERE ARE MY SCREEN CAPTURES STORED? If you press the volume Up/Down button to capture screenshots on your PlayBook, you can find these images saved in the Camera Pictures album.

After selecting an album and tapping a photo to view it, you can perform the following while viewing photos:

+ Zoom in and out while viewing. You can pinch apart or together to control zooming within a picture. If you double tap then a default zoom level will toggle in and out.

DOUBLE-TAP ON DIFFERENT AREAS You can double-tap on different areas of the photo to dynamically zoom into different parts of your photo; the zoom actually zooms into the specific area where you tap your finger. Double-tapping again takes you back out to the full photo view.

+ Swipe left or right to move between pictures in your album.

+ To delete a photo, swipe down from the top frame to the display, and tap Delete. Tap Delete again to confirm your intended action.

+ Swipe down from the top frame towards the center of the display and select to Set as Wallpaper for a photo you want to use as your Home screen wallpaper.

+ To play your photos in a slideshow, simply tap on a photo and tap the Right Arrow/Play button. You cannot control the speed of the slideshow, but the default is 3 seconds.

VIEWING ONLY, NO EDITING You cannot perform any editing of your photos with the default Photos application on your PlayBook. There are third-party applications available that give you the ability to edit your photos, such as TouchUp Pro and Photo Effects Sharing.

Sharing Your Pictures

Now that you have transferred photos to your PlayBook or used it to capture photos, you will want to share them with family and friends. To do so, you can send them via email or via photo programs in the web browser or even show them off on an HD TV or display.

SHARE PHOTOS VIA EMAIL

You cannot share your photos via email from within the Pictures or Camera applications, but you can attach them to email through the BlackBerry Bridge and a connected BlackBerry smartphone. Read Chapter 6 (How Can I Read and Use Email on My PlayBook?) to see how to attach photos to your email.

SHARE PHOTOS VIA THE WEB BROWSER

Because of the powerful web browser on the PlayBook, you can attach photos to your email through the browser and your web-based email client. You can also upload them to Facebook, Twitter, and various other social networking and photo management websites through the web browser just like you would from a PC or Mac. Simply visit your preferred service, and use the browse function to browse to your PlayBook photos for selection to upload, as shown in Figure 10-19.

FIGURE 10-19 Browsing for a photo from within the browser

SHARE PHOTOS VIA HDMI

You can enjoy sharing photos and running photo slideshows while visiting friends, relatives, or even giving a presentation thanks to the PlayBook and HMDI native support. To share via HDMI, simply connect the HDMI cable to your PlayBook's HDMI port, and then launch the Pictures application. When you connect via HDMI to your TV, you see exactly what is shown on your PlayBook display projected to the external monitor or TV that you connect to.

Related Questions

✦ Where are the two cameras physically located on my PlayBook?
PAGES 5 AND 9

✦ Where can I read more about the web browser and how it works?
PAGE 60

✦ Where can I check the HDMI settings? **PAGE 268**

CHAPTER ELEVEN

WHAT APPS DO I HAVE AND HOW CAN I GET MORE?

In this chapter:

+ Using Your Preloaded Apps
+ Finding, Downloading, and Installing Apps via BlackBerry App World

Various chapters throughout this book cover applications preloaded on your PlayBook, but this chapter covers those "extra" default applications. These applications are still extremely useful, fun, and full-featured. In addition, this chapter explains how you can install a growing number of third-party applications from BlackBerry App World directly to your PlayBook.

Using Your Preloaded Apps

Your PlayBook comes preloaded with many applications, so you can get up-and-running without having to visit BlackBerry App World to enjoy them. Most of these applications are a part of the operating system and cannot be removed from your PlayBook, but you can move the icons around the Home screen. Preloaded apps not covered in other chapters include Weather, Bing Maps, Need for Speed, Tetris, Calculator, and Clock, so now take a look at these in more detail.

WEATHER

Weather on the BlackBerry PlayBook is powered by AccuWeather.com and is an attractive and capable application that presents all the essential information you need on the large display, as shown in Figure 11-1, including the following:

+ Location and basic forecast (rain, snow, and sun)
+ Current temperature
+ Temperature and condition forecast for the next several hours
+ Wind direction and speed
+ Times for sunrise and sunset
+ Web browser link to weather maps
+ Link to hourly forecast with RealFeel temperatures and precipitation levels
+ One tap (or swipe) access to the next 5 days

FIGURE 11-1 Weather on the BlackBerry PlayBook

You can easily toggle between Fahrenheit and Celsius and add other locations using the menu accessed by swiping down from the top frame (see Figure 11-2). This upper-menu area can also show you the high and low temperatures and forecast conditions for your other locations in a thumbnail view.

FIGURE 11-2 Upper menu and locations

To add another location to your weather database, follow these steps:

1. Swipe down from the upper frame to access the menu.
2. Tap the large Gear icon on the far left. The temperature toggle (F/C) appears with a + icon to the right of it.
3. Tap the + icon to add another location. A text box with Add a City above it appears.
4. Enter the name of the city you want to add; then tap the Return button to have the application search the database for the city and give you some matches.
5. Tap the + to the right of the city you want to add, and it appears in full-screen view with all the latest weather details.

When you have more than one location loaded, you can swipe up or down on the center of the display to scroll between locations. You can also swipe down from the upper frame and scroll between locations with the thumbnail view.

BING MAPS

Your BlackBerry PlayBook comes with an integrated GPS receiver application for mapping and navigating called Bing Maps. You need an active Wi-Fi connection to use Bing Maps because it is not an offline navigation application. After Bing Maps launches you see options on the left for getting directions, viewing traffic, and viewing businesses (see Figure 11-3). Tap on one of these options to perform the indicated action or search Bing by entering text in the Search Box in the upper left of Bing Maps. Many of the options lead to multiple choices and actions, which are as follows:

* **Get Directions**: Tap this button and a pop-up appears in the left column with icons for Drive, Transit, or Walking Directions with an A and B entry field. Add more stops to car and walking routes by tapping the Add to Route option. There are check boxes for avoiding highways, avoiding toll roads, and making a round trip, as shown in Figure 11-4. The transit option enables you to specify when you want to depart or arrive. Tap Settings, to see buttons for miles or km and an option to save your destination history. Enter your points, tap the Get Directions button, and your route appears in the left column in text and as a blue path on the map (see Figure 11-5).

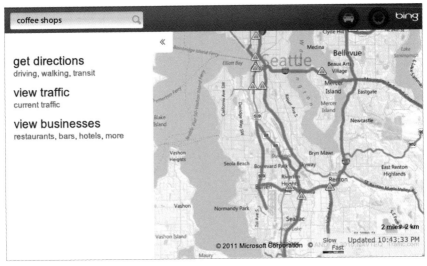

FIGURE 11-3 Bing Maps main display

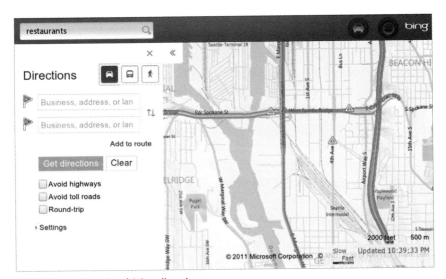

FIGURE 11-4 Entering driving directions

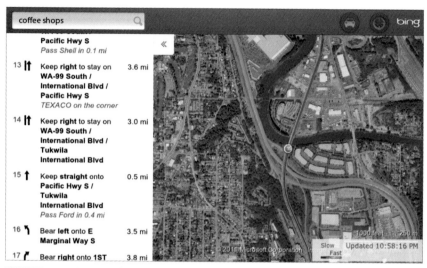

FIGURE 11-5 Directions for your trip

✤ **View Traffic**: Tap this option to toggle traffic on and off. Traffic appears with colors on the main roads such that green is clear and black is backed up.

✤ **View Businesses**: Tap this option to view business categories; then browse to find places that interest you, as shown in Figure 11-6 for movie theaters. You can find some quick business filter buttons in the upper right after swiping down from the upper frame, including coffee shops, restaurants, and bars. You can also change the map view by swiping down to reveal the menu and then selecting from Auto, Road, Aerial, or Bird's Eye (see Figure 11-7).

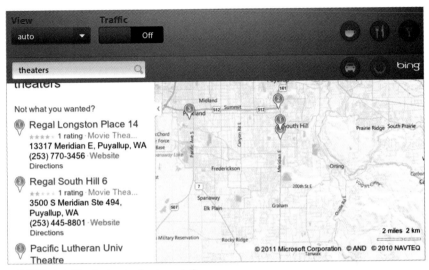

FIGURE 11-6 Movie theater business info

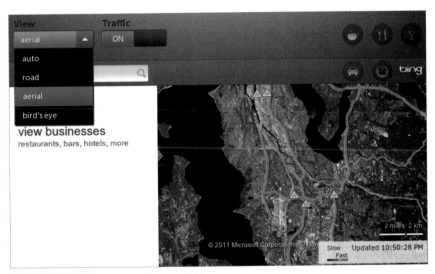

FIGURE 11-7 Different map views available

NEED FOR SPEED UNDERCOVER AND TETRIS

Two games are installed on your PlayBook out-of-the box: *Need for Speed Undercover* and *Tetris*. You do have the option to uninstall these games, but after playing both of them, you will probably want to leave them on your PlayBook. These games are written with the PlayBook Native Development Kit (NDK) and you can immediately tell because they are both extremely high quality and provide fantastic game play.

Need for Speed Undercover

Need for Speed Undercover is a fast-paced racing game designed specifi-cally for an optimized experience on the BlackBerry PlayBook. You can find options for customizing your car, including making game-play purchases for performance and appearance in the virtual shop, as shown Figure 11-8. The goals of the game change as you move through the different levels and specific instructions are provided. Sometimes you need to place in first or second; other times you need to outrun the police; and in others you need to take out the bad guys. You get points and game play money (see Figure 11-9) for wins, close calls, nudges, and other tricks and moves during the driving experience.

FIGURE 11-8 Buying items in the shop

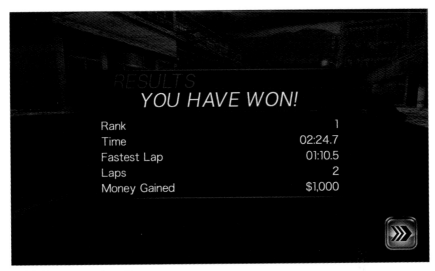

FIGURE 11-9 Winning a Race

NO ACCELERATION CONTROL You can brake in *NFS Undercover*, but there is no accelerator to worry about. You can accelerate automatically, and the longer you go without hitting something, the faster you will go.

Make sure to go through the tutorial to learn all about handling your car. Tilt your PlayBook right and left to steer, swipe up the display for nitro, swipe down for braking, and more. It is an interactive experience, and the graphics and gameplay are fluid on the PlayBook.

Tetris

After you launch *Tetris* you can see your display automatically rotate to portrait orientation, unless you are already in this orientation. *Tetris* is a classic puzzle game and is optimized and designed to only be played in portrait orientation. The main Home screen for *Tetris* includes options for the following, as shown in Figure 11-10.

FIGURE 11-10 Main *Tetris* screen

+ **Marathon**: This is the classic game where you try to gain as many points as you can while you clear 150 lines across 15 levels.

ENDLESS MARATHON If you complete level 15, you enter the Endless Marathon mode where there are NO limits to levels and even extra difficulty.

+ **Magic**: This game mode is played over 15 levels with a different line goal in each level.

+ **Statistics**: Tap this selection to see stats on your gameplay such as total time played, number of games played, high scores, and highest level completed.

+ **Options**: Tap this selection to view choices for controlling game options (ghost piece and reset game), ambiance options (volume, music, and sound effects), and viewing the game tutorials.

✦ **Help & About**: This selection gives you access to all the game help documentation, as shown in Figure 11-11.

✦ **Quick Play**: This selection enables you to jump right into where you left your last saved game or start a new Marathon game if you have no current saved games, as shown in Figure 11-12.

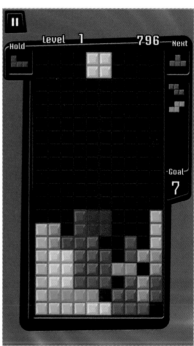

FIGURE 11-11 Help & About page

FIGURE 11-12 Playing a game via Quick Play

Tetris on the PlayBook is fully controlled by touch, with these supported actions:

✦ Drag left or right to move left or right.

✦ Tap the right side of the display to rotate clockwise.

✦ Tap the left side of the display to rotate counter-clockwise.

✦ Drag down to execute a soft drop.

✦ Swipe down for a hard drop.

✦ Swipe up or tap the Hold zone in the upper left to put a block (aka Tetrimino) on hold. This switches to another form of block coming down at you.

If you don't play *Tetris* often, the ghost piece is helpful; when in use, a faded piece appears down below in the stack that dynamically changes as you rotate your block. You can turn off the ghost piece option if you prefer more of a challenge. Additionally, there are special items in the Magic mode and special moves such as multiple line clears and T-spins. Explore the game tutorials to find out more about enjoying *Tetris* on the PlayBook.

CALCULATOR

RIM includes a calculator on the PlayBook optimized for the display with large buttons for easy operation. Like some of these other applications, the calculator operates only in landscape orientation. The calculator has four modes:

+ Standard
+ Scientific
+ Unit Converter
+ Tip Calculator

To access these different modes, swipe down from the top frame after launching the calculator app (see Figure 11-13).

FIGURE 11-13 Different calculator modes

Standard Mode

When you launch the calculator application, you start in standard mode, as shown in Figure 11-14, where you can find all the basics, including the following:

+ Numbers 0–9
+ Common operators (addition, subtraction, division, and multiplication)
+ Percentage
+ Square root
+ Squared

+ Parentheses for controlling calculation order

+ Memory options (memory in, memory out, clear, and recall)

+ Enter, clear, and backspace

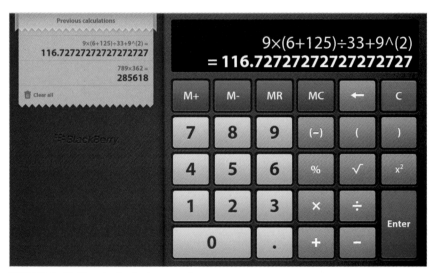

FIGURE 11-14 Standard calculator mode

- -

IMPROPER ENTRY WARNING If you try to enter an invalid argument in the equation, you see a red background flash in the calculator display box and your entry does not register.

- -

As you enter your calculation, it appears in the black display area with your result in bold above the buttons. After you complete a calculation and press Enter, your calculation appears on the left in the previous calculations area where your last seven calculations are listed for reference. You can also tap once to clear out this list of previous calculations.

- -

CALCULATOR ANIMATIONS ARE SLICK When you clear all your previous calculations, a torn piece of virtual paper appears to fly off to the right of your display.

- -

Scientific Mode

The standard mode likely meets the needs of most people, but there is also a scientific mode available for more indepth calculations. As you can see in Figure 11-15, the scientific mode has an extensive list of additional functions and takes up the entire width of the display. If you tap on the FN button you see 12 more alternative functions appear. To access previous calculations in scientific mode, tap the top of the display where it shows an arrow next to the words Previous Calculations.

FIGURE 11-15 Scientific mode enabled

Unit Converter

The unit converter is controlled by three columns on the left of the display where you choose your data type, known unit, and unknown unit, as shown in Figure 11-16. There are data types for the following:

+ Angle
+ Area
+ Data
+ Energy
+ Length

✛ Power

✛ Pressure

✛ Speed

✛ Temperature

✛ Time

✛ Volume

✛ Weight

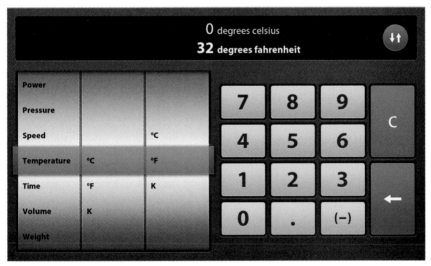

FIGURE 11-16 Unit converter is active.

Within each of these data types are a significant number of units to select from. The process to perform a conversion is as follows:

1. Select a data type from the left column.

2. Select the known/given unit from the center column.

3. Select the unit you want to determine from the right column.

4. Using the number pad, enter the quantity of the known unit you want to convert. You see the known quantity appear in the black display area with the conversion result below it in bold font.

ONE TAP FOR INVERSE CONVERSION Tap the Double Arrow icon on the right in the black display area to switch the given and unknown units. The entered value you previously input remains the same, but the units switch between the two arguments.

Tip Calculator

After checking out the slick Tip Calculator on the PlayBook, (see Figure 11-17) you may decide you need your PlayBook with you for all future restaurant meals.

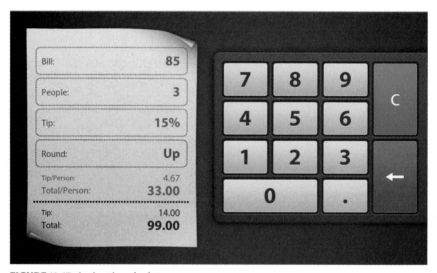

FIGURE 11-17 Active tip calculator

The fields on the left side are for the following:

✦ **Bill**: Here is where you enter in the total amount of your bill.

✦ **People**: Enter in the number of people who will be splitting the bill.

✦ **Tip**: Enter the % tip you want to leave for your wait staff.

✦ **Round**: Choose to round up (if you don't want to deal with coin change) or not at all. The tip calculator rounds to the nearest half dollar.

✦ **Tip/Person and Total/Person**: These two lines break down the tip and total per person at your table.

✦ **Tip**: Here is where you can find the total calculated tip.

✦ **Total**: This is the total of your bill plus the calculated tip.

The right side consists of the numbers 0–9, a decimal, clear button, and backspace button.

MORE THAN JUST FOR RESTAURANTS Don't forget you can use the tip calculator to figure out the tip for any transaction, including a cab ride, cruise ship staff, bar tab, and more.

CLOCK

Another included application is the Clock, which actually consists of three different utilities in one: a clock/alarm, stopwatch, and timer (see Figure 11-18). To switch between these three, swipe your finger from right to left and back again. You will see that you are able to scroll through all three; to access and use one of the utilities, simply tap it when you see it appear in the center of your display.

FIGURE 11-18 Three main clock modes

Clock/Alarm

The clock utility has a tab for both Clock and Alarm, as shown in Figure 11-19.
Controls for the clock part include the following:

+ **Name of the clock:** The text above it reflects whatever you enter here.

+ **Time zone selector**: Choose your time zone.

+ **Clock face**: Choose from analog or digital.

FIGURE 11-19 Clock options

If you then tap the Alarm tab, you see these options, shown in Figure 11-20:

+ **Roller dial:** Set the time of the alarm.

+ **Alarm:** Toggle for on or off.

+ **Repeat:** Tap on a day of the week to set.

+ **Sound:** Choose from evolving, traditional, or none.

+ **Snooze:** Choose 0–30 minutes in various increments.

NO CUSTOM ALARM SOUNDS Unfortunately, there is no way to preview the alarm sound or choose a custom sound or a song from your music collection.

FIGURE 11-20 Setting up an alarm

If you swipe down from the top frame after switching back into the scroll mode, you see the ability to add a new clock and a toggle for the date. You can add several new clocks and alarms, but no new stopwatch or timer. If you are traveling you may want to have different clocks set up on different time zones.

Stopwatch

Your stopwatch is simply a large dial with Start/Stop and Reset buttons underneath it. If you continue to press Start without resetting, you see the right button change to Lap, so you can tap that when a lap is complete (refer back to Figure 11-18). You see that elapsed time is in tenths of seconds.

Timer

The timer looks similar to the stopwatch with the large white face and time status to the tenth of a second. Tap on the timer face to see roller dial selectors for hours and minutes that you can use to set up your countdown timer, as shown in Figure 11-21. Sound selections include evolving, traditional, or none. Tap Start to begin the timer countdown.

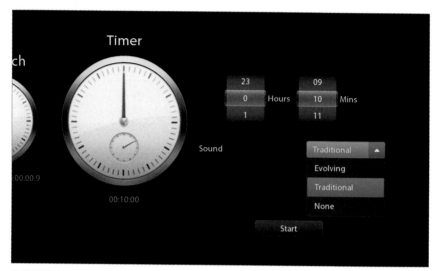

FIGURE 11-21 Setting up the timer

Finding, Downloading, and Installing Apps via BlackBerry App World

As you read in Chapter 1 (What Is a BlackBerry PlayBook?), one thing that currently sets other tablets apart from the PlayBook is the number of available applications. The number has increased significantly since launch with 1,750 apps after one week to more than 3,000 a month later. RIM released more development tools at the beginning of May 2011, so you should see more and better quality applications coming to the BlackBerry PlayBook via BlackBerry App World.

BROWSE AND SEARCH FOR APPS

When you launch BlackBerry App World on the PlayBook, you see the main featured page, as shown in Figure 11-22. A select number of featured apps appear with large icons in the top half of your display.

FIGURE 11-22 Main BlackBerry App World page

Tap the arrow to the right under these large thumbnails to shrink them down and reveal 25 application icons (five columns and three rows) in each of the following four main categories (see Figure 11-23):

+ Newest
+ Top Free
+ Top Purchased
+ Recently Updated

FIGURE 11-23 Seeing more featured apps

In the upper left of the BlackBerry App World, you can find three main browsing options: Featured, Categories, and My World. Tap the Categories option to see 19 categories, as shown in Figure 11-24. You can also find subcategories within these main categories that further define the applications (see Figure 11-25). When you get to a page of applications, you can find filters in the top right for all paid and free apps.

FIGURE 11-24 Application categories

FIGURE 11-25 A typical subcategory

You can spend hours browsing through all the subcategories trying to discover apps, or if you know what you are looking for, simply search for it. The search box is found in the top right of BlackBerry App World. Enter a name for an app, and tap the Return button to search. Results appear on a single page organized into five columns (see Figure 11-26).

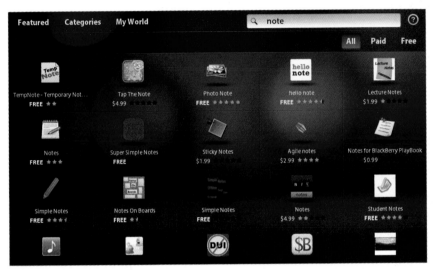

FIGURE 11-26 Search results for "note"

DOWNLOAD AND INSTALL APPS

After you find an application that interests you, tap on the Thumbnail icon to see more about the application. The specific application page shows you the following (see Figure 11-27):

+ **Upper left**: Name, developer, version, size, and rating.
+ **Lower left**: Screenshots of the application where you can access more by swiping right and left.
+ **Upper right**: Text descriptions and details about the application.
+ **Lower right**: Reviews of the application. Tap the More Reviews hyperlink to see the entire right column change into a column of reviews, assuming that there are enough reviews to fill the column. If there are more reviews than a single column, you can swipe up and down to access more.

FIGURE 11-27 Typical application page

When you make the final decision to download an app, tap the Download button. The application downloads and installs automatically and then appears in the My World tab. Tap My World in the upper left to see all the apps you have installed (see Figure 11-28). You can see the installed version number and a button to delete it from your PlayBook.

FIGURE 11-28 Apps installed on my PlayBook

If you want to leave a review for an application you have installed, follow these steps:

1. Tap the application in the My World tab to open up the specific application page (refer to Figure 11-28).

2. Tap the Add Review button in the lower right below the description, see Figure 11-29. A page appears with options to write a review.

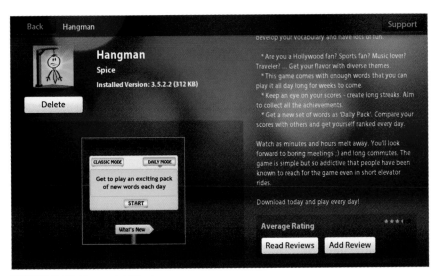

FIGURE 11-29 Tap on Add Review.

3. Enter a title for your review, text of your review, and tap a rating (from 1 to 5 stars) (see Figure 11-30).

4. Tap the Submit Review button to post your application review.

To remove an application from your PlayBook, follow these steps:

1. From the My World Installed list, tap the Delete button. A confirmation pop-up appears.

2. Confirm your intention by tapping Delete again.

3. The app will be deleted and appear in your list of uninstalled applications.

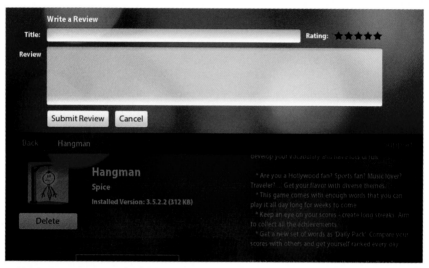

FIGURE 11-30 Enter text for your review.

- -

WHAT ARE UNAVAILABLE APPS Because you use your BlackBerry ID on both your PlayBook and your smartphone, there will be applications you have on your smartphone that are not available for the PlayBook. These applications appear on the Unavailable page of your PlayBook.

- -

Related Questions

✦ How can I move application icons around on the Home screen? **PAGE 44**

✦ Can I use the web browser to find apps? **PAGE 60**

✦ Can I install apps through a desktop connection? **PAGE 276**

CHAPTER TWELVE

HOW CAN I READ EBOOKS ON MY PLAYBOOK?

In this chapter:

+ Using the Kobo eReading Application
+ Using Adobe Reader

O n May 19, 2011, Amazon announced that it officially sold more eBooks than hardcover and paperback books combined (`http://phx.corporate-ir .net/phoenix.zhtml?ID=1565581&c=176060&p=irol-newsArticle`). You can now carry multiple titles in a single device, save your place in a book across multiple devices, purchase new books on the go, and reduce the use of paper for books. Amazon also announced that a Kindle eBook application will be launching on the BlackBerry PlayBook, but for now the ability to read eBooks comes with the Kobo eReading application and Adobe Reader for PDF titles.

Using the Kobo eReading Application

Kobo is an eBook retailer backed by several technology leaders including Indigo Books and Music. You can access more than 2.3 million eBook titles, all open-source. Thus, when you purchase eBook titles from the Kobo store, you can read them not only on your BlackBerry PlayBook but also on dedicated eBook readers, smartphones, your PC, and more.

TRY USING KOBO IN PORTRAIT Rotating your BlackBerry PlayBook into portrait orientation gives you an experience closer to a physical book, and the layout of eBooks is much better in this orientation. As you can see in screenshots in this chapter, Kobo is optimized for portrait orientation.

BUYING EBOOKS

The two main parts of the Kobo eReading application on your PlayBook are the store front and your library. Kobo does not support loading EPUB-formatted eBooks from your PC at this time; thus, all titles must be purchased from the Kobo storefront. If you purchase titles from your PC or another eBook device, they will all be available to you as soon as you sign into your Kobo account on the PlayBook.

YOU MUST BE 13 YEARS OLD The Kobo terms of usage state that you must be at least 13 years old to sign up for an account, so if you are younger than this, make sure your parents help you get your PlayBook setup.

To start with Kobo on your PlayBook, follow these steps:

1. Find the Kobo Books application icon on your Home screen, either in the All or Media tabs, and tap it to launch the application.

2. Tap the left option to sign in and create an account, as shown in Figure 12-1.

3. If you have an account, you can sign in with your email and password and tap the Sign In button. If you do not have an account, tap the Get Started button (see Figure 12-2).

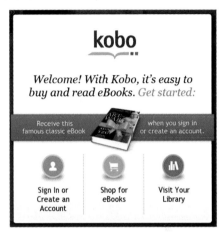

FIGURE 12-1 Initial startup of Kobo on the PlayBook

4. Enter your email address and create a password at least six characters long (see Figure 12-3). You can slide the toggle for newsletters and special offers from Yes to No if you want.

5. Tap the Create Account button. Your account will be created, and Kobo launches you into the store front (see Figure 12-4) with you signed into your account.

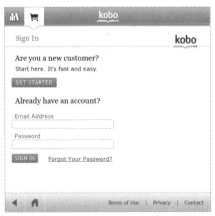

FIGURE 12-2 Create an account or sign into Kobo.

FIGURE 12-3 Enter an email address and password for a new account.

Now that you have an account or are signed into an existing account, you can browse through the bookstore to find something to read. As you saw in Figure 12-4, the home page for the Kobo store in portrait orientation shows the latest new releases on the top, the top 50 below that, and popular categories on the bottom. There is a search box in the upper right above new releases that enables you to search for a specific title. Quick navigation buttons also appear in the upper right above the search box for the following:

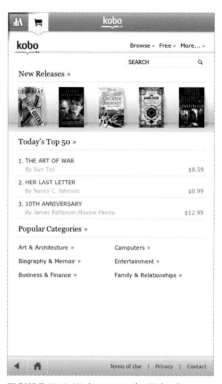

FIGURE 12-4 Welcome to the Kobo Store

- **Browse**: As shown in Figure 12-5, this button takes you to all the categories in the store, not just the most popular. Tap one of these to see all the books in that category to browse through with the title, author, rating, cover, and price, as shown by the Sci Fi & Fantasy section in Figure 12-6.

EXISTING ACCOUNT LOGIN BRINGS YOU YOUR LIBRARY If you sign in with an existing account, all the books that you previously purchased start to download to your PlayBook. You can visit your library page and tap and hold on each book title to choose to remove it from your library, or pause the download for later usage if you do not want all of them on your PlayBook.

FIGURE 12-5 Browsing by category   **FIGURE 12-6** Sci Fi & Fantasy category

➕ **Free**: Tap the Free option to view pages of free eBooks that you can download for no cost (see Figure 12-7).

➕ **More**: Tapping More takes you to a page of recommended reading (see Figure 12-8) that has various book categories such as the following, plus many more:

➕ NYT Fiction Bestsellers

➕ As Seen on TV

➕ Oprah's Book Club

➕ Christian Living

➕ Kid's Picks

➕ Spy Games

➕ Life Lessons

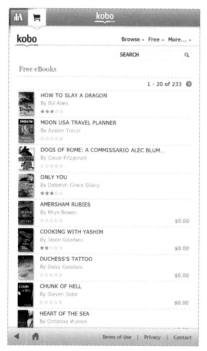

FIGURE 12-7 Free eBooks in the Kobo Store

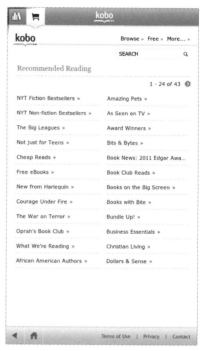

FIGURE 12-8 Recommended reading categories

When you find a title that interests you, tap it to open up that specific book page (see Figure 12-9). You can see the name of the book, the rating, price, author, language, and book synopsis. If you tap Get Preview, part of the book, typically part of the first chapter, downloads to your library as a free sample.

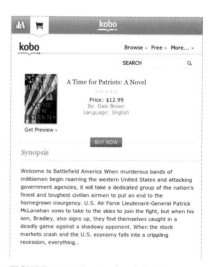

FIGURE 12-9 Viewing book details

Once you have navigated to the specific book page that you want to purchase, follow these steps to complete the transaction for the book:

1. Tap the green Buy Now button when you find a book you want to purchase.

2. A page with your payment information appears. Tap the Buy Now button to make the book purchase (see Figure 12-10). If you do not yet have a credit card number associated with your account, you can enter it here.

3. After confirming your purchase details, the purchase takes place on your PlayBook, and your book downloads to your library immediately, ready for you to begin reading.

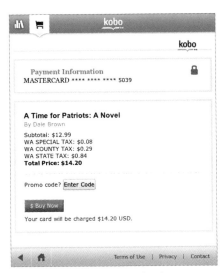

FIGURE 12-10 Purchasing a book

PROMO CODE FOR BOOK PURCHASES You may receive promo codes from time-to-time if you sign up for the Kobo newsletter. Tap the Promo Code button, enter it into the box, and tap the Apply button to apply the discount code to your purchase.

READING EBOOKS

Now that you have eBooks in your library, you can enjoy them on your PlayBook. To switch the view from the store to the library, tap the Library icon (shown as book ends in the upper-left corner) to view your library (refer to Figure 12-4). In your library, you can view the book covers of your purchased titles on the shelf in the default grid view (see Figure 12-11). You can also view your library titles in list view (see Figure 12-12) by tapping the Double Arrow icon on the left side of your library view followed by the List View icon in the lower left of the index that slides out (see Figure 12-13).

FIGURE 12-11 Viewing your library in grid view

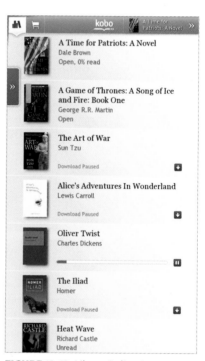

FIGURE 12-12 Library in list view

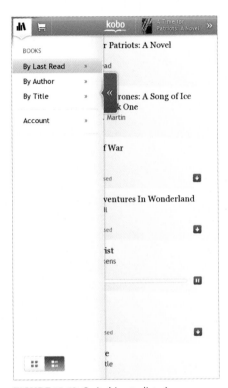

FIGURE 12-13 Switching to list view

SORT YOUR LIBRARY As you can see in the slide that comes out on the left side of your page in Figure 12-13, you have quick tap options to view your library by last read, author, or title.

To open up a book to read, tap the book in your library. Your selected book title then opens in full screen mode for your reading pleasure. Don't just settle for the default reading mode though; tap in the center of the display of your open book title to see the following controls appear in a top menu bar, as shown in Figure 12-14.

+ **Library:** Tap the top-left Book-ends icon to jump back to your library.

+ **Reading mode:** Tap the open book icon when you are in another mode to return to reading your book.

✦ **Table of contents**: Tap the list icon to view the table of contents, as shown in Figure 12-15. From here you can tap on a chapter or other location in the table of contents and jump to that part of your book.

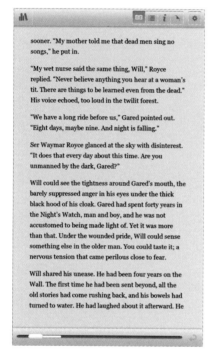

FIGURE 12-14 Book options

FIGURE 12-15 Table of contents

✦ **Book overview**: Tap on the small i to see the overview of your selected book, as shown in Figure 12-16. Here you will see the book cover, rating, title, author, and a description of the book.

✦ **Dogear**: Tap the folded page corner to view a list of the dogears you have created; tap one in the list to go to that page (see Figure 12-17). To create a dogear, simply tap the upper-right corner of your book as you read it. To clear a dogear, tap the upper-right corner again.

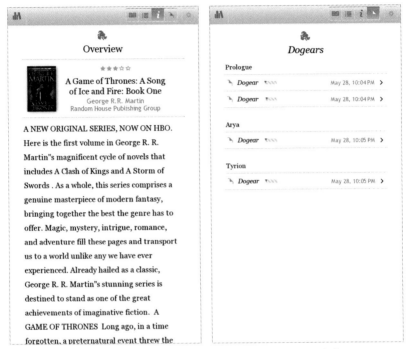

FIGURE 12-16 Overview of your book   **FIGURE 12-17** Dogears index

- **Settings:** Tap the gear icon in the far right corner once to see more options to customize your reading experience appear in the bottom of the display (see Figure 12-18):

  - **Font settings**: Use the slider bar to choose from nine different font sizes and the drop-down list to choose from two font styles.

  - **Display settings**: There is a toggle to turn night mode on or off and a slider bar to adjust the brightness of the display, as shown in Figure 12-19. When night mode is enabled the text appears in white with a black background (see Figure 12-20).

  - **Reading settings**: Tap on reading settings to see options to control the page transition (fade or slide) (see Figure 12-21) and landscape layout (single or double page).

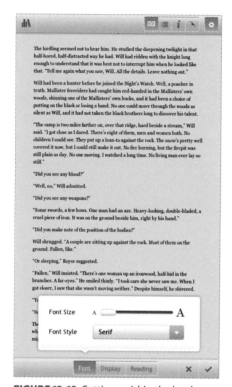

FIGURE 12-18 Settings within the book

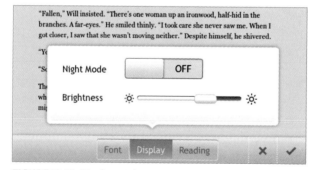

FIGURE 12-19 Display settings

FIGURE 12-20 Night mode enabled

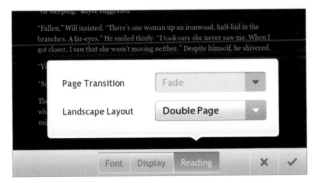

FIGURE 12-21 Reading settings

✦ **Page navigation slider**: A slider bar appears along the bottom of the page you are reading that you can drag left and right to navigate quickly through your book. As you slide the bar, the specific location where you are appears in a pop-up box (see Figure 12-22).

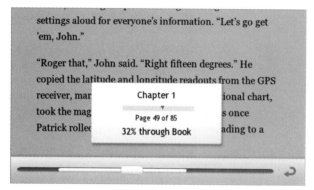

FIGURE 12-22 Navigation slider bar

TOUCH AND HOLD LIBRARY OPTIONS If you touch and hold on a book in your library, you can see options to Read Now, Resume This Download, Pause This Download, and Remove from Library.

Now that you have your reading experience customized to how you like it, you can start reading. Simply swipe from right to left to turn to the next page or tap the right 1/3 of the page. You can also go back to a previous page in the book by sliding left to right or tapping on the left side.

Using Adobe Reader

RIM includes a PDF reader with the Adobe Reader application. Follow these steps to launch and start using the application to read a PDF:

1. After launching the application by tapping the Adobe Acrobat icon on your Home screen, you see a file explorer page appear, as shown in Figure 12-23.

FIGURE 12-23 Looking for a PDF file to view

2. Tap a PDF file stored on your PlayBook or connected BlackBerry smartphone.

3. Tap the Open button to view it in Adobe Reader.

The Adobe Reader is quick and simple to use. Swiping down from the top frame reveals the following information, as shown in Figure 12-24:

◆ **Title:** Name of the document you have open.

◆ **File Folder**: The icon in the top right takes you back to the file explorer page if you tap it.

◆ **Page slider bar**: You can slide the box along the slider at the bottom of the page to move to different pages in your document. On the left above the slider bar, you can see the page number where you are over the total of page numbers in the document.

FIGURE 12-24 Options in the PDF file

PINCH TO ZOOM IN AND OUT Although your document may appear small when you first open it up, remember you can use the same pinch together and apart actions to zoom in and out on your document.

The Adobe Reader application works in both landscape and portrait orientations. In portrait your document appears with a full single page appearing on the display. Swipe left and right to navigate through your document. In landscape your document page is split into a top and bottom view. Swipe up and down, in addition to left and right, to navigate your document in this orientation.

Related Questions

✤ How do I use gestures to turn a page or zoom in on a PDF? **PAGES 43 AND 45**

✤ How do I find any other eBook reader apps available? **PAGE 216**

CHAPTER THIRTEEN

HOW DO I KEEP MY PLAYBOOK SECURE?

In this chapter:

+ Managing Application Permissions
+ Using Certificates
+ Switching into Development Mode
+ Set, Enable, and Change Your Password
+ Perform a Security Wipe
+ Manage Your VPN Profiles

R IM helps you keep your PlayBook secure by requiring a BlackBerry Bridge setup for access to your email, calendar, and contacts, but you can also manage other specific security settings to control access on your PlayBook. Some settings are available within specific applications, but RIM also provides a central area for security management within your PlayBook settings area.

Managing Application Permissions

You can find settings within some applications by swiping down from the upper frame and viewing what is available on the menu. You can find settings related to security issues pertaining to applications such as file sharing, camera integration, device identification, and GPS location, within the settings area of your PlayBook. You won't find every application here in the security area; just those that have the potential to share information off of the PlayBook. To access your application permissions security area, follow these steps:

1. From the Home screen, tap the gear icon in the upper-right.

2. In the left column of this settings area, swipe up until you see the security setting and tap it. A list of available security settings appears on the right side of your display (see Figure 13-1).

FIGURE 13-1 Available security settings

3. Tap the Application Permissions setting in the list of security settings. A list of your different applications with manageable security settings appears, as show in Figure 13-2.

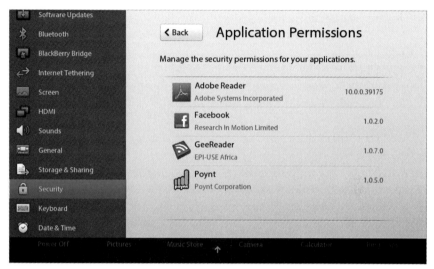

FIGURE 13-2 Application permissions page

To access the security settings for an application in the Application Permissions list, tap the application. The following list provides three examples of applications and their security settings.

✦ **Adobe Reader** (PDF reader detailed in Chapter 12 [How Can I Read Ebooks on My PlayBook?]): Tap on this Application icon to view the Files access settings that you can manage (see Figure 13-3). Choose from Allowed, Denied, and Prompt. The default is Allowed. Denied does not allow access, whereas Prompt gives you a choice for each specific file.

✦ **Facebook** (PlayBook Facebook application): Facebook has both Files and Camera access settings (see Figure 13-4). The Permission Details page states that your camera could potentially be used to detect your surroundings, giving cause for security options. Again, options for these two settings are Allowed, Denied, and Prompt.

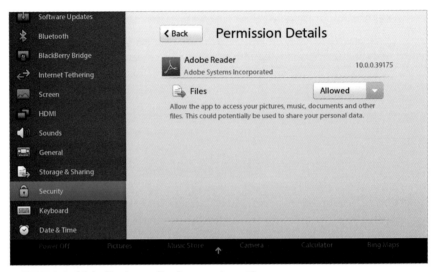

FIGURE 13-3 Adobe Reader application security settings

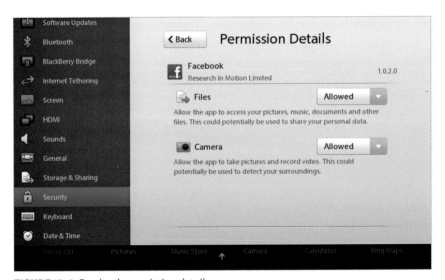

FIGURE 13-4 Facebook permission details

✦ **Poynt** (Location-based application): Poynt has security permission settings for device identifying information and GPS location (see Figure 13-5). Poynt is an application that pairs with your BlackBerry smartphone to provide an enhanced user experience, so your device information is used to make that pairing. Because the application uses your GPS to show you movies, restaurants, gas prices, and more based on your location, there are permission settings for GPS location.

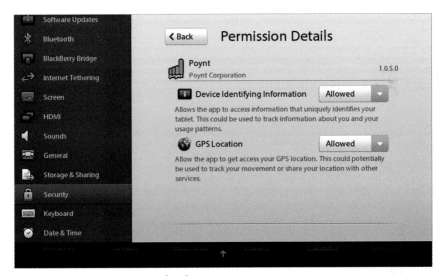

FIGURE 13-5 Poynt permission details

In most cases, people leave these application security settings on the default setting. If you have security concerns, visit this area of your settings and manage them as you want. If Denied is your selected option, the application does not function as designed and closes when you try to perform the action that is denied.

- -

HOW DOES A PROMPT FUNCTION? As you can see in Figure 13-6, if you select the Prompt option, a pop-up appears informing you what the application is requesting to do. Tap the OK button to accept the request or close out of the application if you do not want to proceed. The pop-up also shows the path to access your settings and change the default setting.

FIGURE 13-6 Prompt pop-up notice

Using Certificates

You can use certificates to manage secure access to websites, email hosts, and more. Many common certificates are included on the PlayBook, but you can also import your own if necessary. To access, view, and manage your certificates, follow these steps:

1. From the Home screen, tap the gear icon in the upper-right.

2. In the left column of this settings area, swipe up until you can see the security setting, and tap it.

3. Tap Certificates from the list of security settings. A list of all of your certificates appears on the page (see Figure 13-7).

4. Tap the drop-down list arrow next to All Certificates to filter by type of certificate. Choose from root, intermediate, and your own.

FIGURE 13-7 List of installed certificates

5. Tap the pencil icon to edit any existing certificates.

6. Tap a certificate name to view the details of the certificate. You can also tap the Trusted box to change the acceptance level of your certificate (see Figure 13-8).

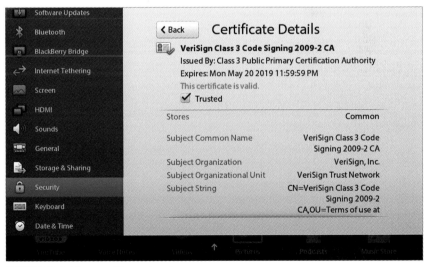

FIGURE 13-8 View certificate details.

Most consumers find the included certificates acceptable for web browsing and have no need for importing their own certificates; however, if you need to access other secure websites or private networks, you can easily transfer certificates over from your home computer to your PlayBook. To do so, follow these steps:

1. Connect your PlayBook to your PC via USB.

2. Locate the security certificate you wish to use on your PC and copy it to the Certificates folder on your PlayBook.

3. Tap the Import button in the lower right of the Certificates screen to walk through the import wizard to select and install the certificate you transferred over from your PC. Figure 13-9 shows the Import Certificates display.

FIGURE 13-9 Import certificates

Switching into Development Mode

As discussed in Chapter 1 (What Is a BlackBerry PlayBook?), a large number of development environments exist on the PlayBook. Developers can enable software development tools on the PlayBook to test out applications, and need to do so before getting approval by RIM and launching on App World.

Through the development mode, developers can side load applications directly from their PC to their PlayBook and try them out. To enable development mode and test an application on your PlayBook, follow these steps:

1. From the Home screen, tap the gear icon in the upper-right.

2. In the left column of this settings area, swipe up until you can see the security setting, and tap it.

3. Tap Development Mode from the list of security settings. A development mode management display appears, as shown in Figure 13-10.

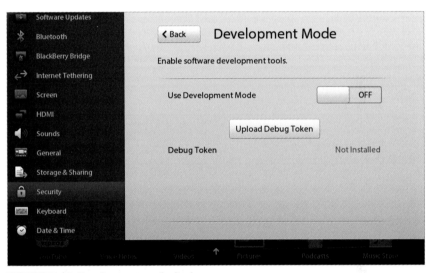

FIGURE 13-10 Development mode display

4. Slide the toggle to the right of the words Use Development Mode. A pop-up appears requiring a device password.

5. Enter a password for your PlayBook twice, and tap the OK button (see Figure 13-11). You can now see that development mode is enabled with an expiration time on the session (defaults to 10 days after you turn on development mode) (see Figure 13-12).

6. Connect your PlayBook to your PC via the USB cable or via Wi-Fi. A pre-installed developer user interface appears, called Playbook Apps Installer program.

FIGURE 13-11 Set your PlayBook password.

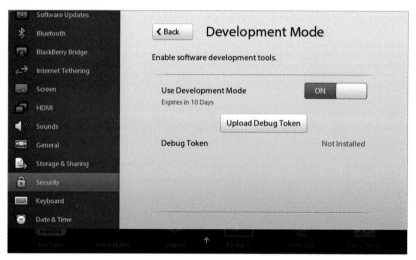

FIGURE 13-12 Development mode is enabled.

7. Enter the IP address and password for your PlayBook. You can find the
   IP address of your PlayBook by viewing the Home screen; a pop-up box
   appears showing that you are currently in development mode and the IP
   address appears in this box (see Figure 13-13).

FIGURE 13-13 IP address available on the Home screen Status bar

8. Select the apps you want to develop; then tap the Install button to install the applications to your PlayBook.

There is also a button to upload a debug token, and after making a connection with your PC, you can upload this token for tracking bugs as you develop applications.

Set, Enable, and Change Your Password

A password can be set on your PlayBook for unlocking your device after a specific period of time, for secure access via Wi-Fi to your PlayBook, and for development mode access (as previously detailed in Chapter 11, [What Apps Do I Have and How Can I Get More?]). To set your password for all three instances, follow these steps:

1. From the Home screen, tap the gear icon in the upper-right.

2. In the left column of this settings area, swipe up until you can see the security setting, and tap on it.

3. Tap on Password from the list of security settings. A password management display appears, as shown in Figure 13-14.

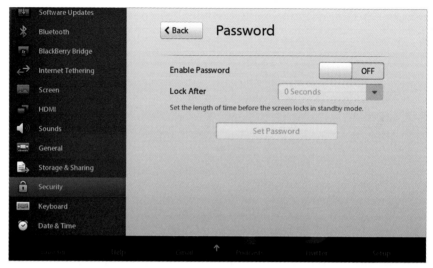

FIGURE 13-14 Main password management display

4. Slide the toggle for Enable Password from the default Off position to On. A pop-up appears for you to enter a new password and confirm the password (see Figure 13-15).

FIGURE 13-15 Set up your password.

5. Enter your new password twice; then tap the OK button to set it on your PlayBook. You are then taken back to the password display where you can select the length of time before the screen locks in standby mode and requires your password, as shown in Figure 13-16.

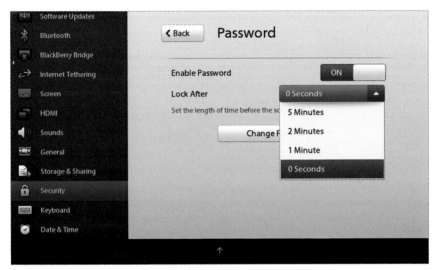

FIGURE 13-16 Password enabled, set the lock time.

6. After your password is set and your display goes into standby mode, you see a prompt appear, as shown in Figure 13-17, when you turn on your display. Enter your password and tap the OK button.

Sometimes, you may want to change your password, and you can do so by tapping the Change Password button. Enter your old password once and new password twice to change your password. If you want to disable the password on your PlayBook, enter your password once to confirm your choice to disable it. The next time you enable the password, you have to enter it twice, just like when you first set up a new password.

- -

WHAT IF I FORGET MY PASSWORD? Try hard to never forget your password because if you enter it wrong 10 times, your PlayBook performs a security wipe and goes back to factory settings.

- -

FIGURE 13-17 Enter a password to unlock your PlayBook.

Perform a Security Wipe

In addition to the involuntary wipe that occurs when you forget your password, RIM also gives you the option to consciously choose to perform a
security wipe. Although necessary at times, performing a security wipe is not
something to take lightly; it will wipe out everything on your device, including
downloaded applications, media, bookmarks, documents, and more. To wipe
your device, follow these steps:

1. From the Home screen, tap the gear icon in the upper-right.

2. In the left column of this settings area, swipe up until you can see the
   security setting, and tap it.

3. Tap Security Wipe from the list of security settings. A security wipe display appears, as shown in Figure 13-18.

4. Enter the word `blackberry` to confirm the security wipe, and then tap
   the Wipe Data button.

FIGURE 13-18 Main security wipe display

You do have the ability to back up your device on your PC, as detailed in Chapter 15 (How Do I Manage My PlayBook with BlackBerry Desktop Software?), and therefore you can restore your PlayBook after a security wipe to the settings you had at the time of your last backup. Be sure to back up often.

Manage Your VPN Profiles

A virtual private network (VPN) is a secure method to connect to a local area network (LAN) remotely from outside of that LAN. For example, you can connect to your work VPN via the PlayBook while you are at home or traveling on the road and have access to your LAN resources and files. To create a new VPN profile on your PlayBook, follow these steps:

1. From the Home screen, tap the gear icon in the upper-right.

2. In the left column of this settings area, swipe up until you can see the security setting, and tap it.

3. Tap VPN from the list of security settings. A VPN management display appears, as shown in Figure 13-19.

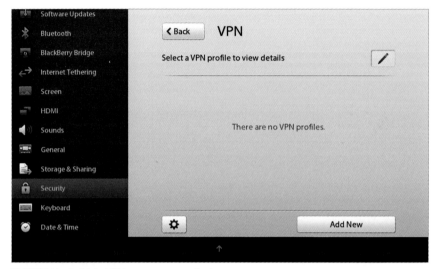

FIGURE 13-19 Main VPN management display

4. Tap the Add New button and the Add New VPN Profile page appears.

5. Fill out all the required information for your particular VPN; check with your network administrator for information about which you are unsure. Figure 13-20 shows an example of these options. You can also tap the Advanced button to see more network specific settings, such as those shown in Figure 13-21.

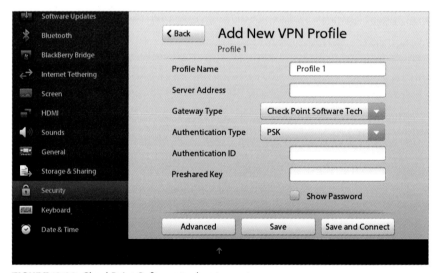

FIGURE 13-20 CheckPoint Software tech gateway type

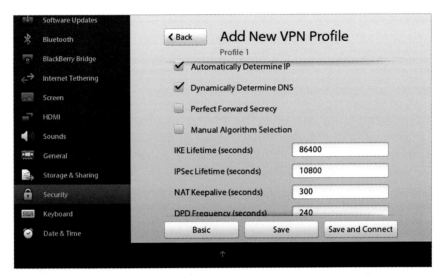

FIGURE 13-21 Some advanced settings

Once you connect to your selected VPN, tap the bottom-left gear icon to view your VPN status (see Figure 13-22). You can also tap the drop-down arrow next to session status in the top right on the status page to view VPN connection logs.

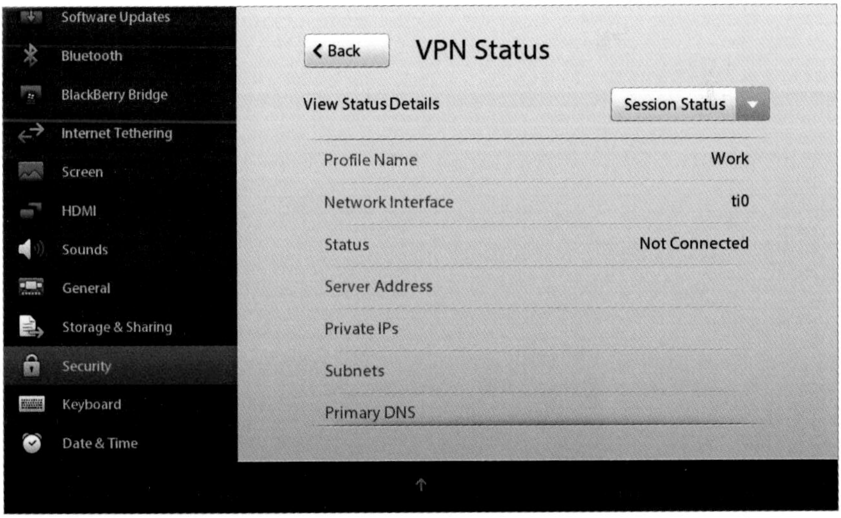

FIGURE 13-22 VPN status page

CHECK WITH YOUR NETWORK ADMINISTRATOR There are too many network specific options to detail in this book for the plethora of gateway and authentication types, so visit your network administrator to find out exactly what you need to set up your VPN profile.

To delete a VPN profile from your list, tap the Pencil icon and then tap the Trash Can icon next to the VPN profile you want to delete (see Figure 13-23). Be careful using this delete action because there is no confirmation of your deletion; tapping the Trash Can immediately deletes your VPN profile. To actually edit your VPN profile, simply tap it from the main VPN profile page, and it opens up in edit mode.

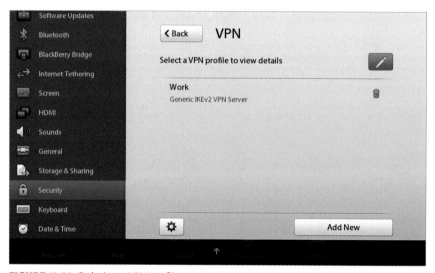

FIGURE 13-23 Deleting a VPN profile

Related Questions

✦ If I wipe out my PlayBook, how do I restore my customized settings?
   PAGE 34

✦ Where can I find applications to install on my PlayBook? **PAGE 216**

✦ How do I back up my data so I won't lose everything in a security wipe? **PAGE 284**

CHAPTER FOURTEEN

HOW DO I MANAGE SETTINGS ON MY PLAYBOOK?

In this chapter:

+ Viewing the About Page
+ Managing Bluetooth Connections
+ Setting Up Internet Tethering
+ Controlling Screen Time-Out and Brightness
+ Setting the HDMI Preferences
+ Managing Your PlayBook Sounds
+ Selecting the General Background Application Settings
+ Managing Your Storage and Sharing Preferences

To ensure the PlayBook experience is consistently great for everyone, RIM gave you the ability to customize the device to your preferences. The best place to do this is in the Settings area, as referenced in many other chapters. Chapter 2 (How Do I Set Up and Customize My PlayBook?) covers customization options such as Wi-Fi settings, BlackBerry Bridge, and the date and time; whereas Chapter 13 (How Do I Keep My PlayBook Secure?) covers the customizable security settings. This chapter discusses in detail more settings to help customize your device to heighten your experience.

Viewing the About Page

You can access the settings area on your PlayBook by tapping on the Gear icon in the far right of the Home screen Status bar or by swiping down from the top frame on the Home screen. The Settings categories are organized in a column on the left side of the display in landscape orientation (see Figure 14-1) and in a list on the top one-third of the display in portrait orientation. The About Page is the first category shown in the list; tap on the word About to access it.

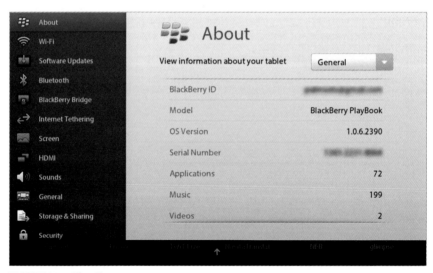

FIGURE 14-1 The About page

The About page presents information about your PlayBook in five catego-ries you can access by tapping the drop-down selector on the right side of the display:

+ **General**: Shows information such as your BlackBerry ID, OS version, number of applications you have installed, and the number of songs and videos you have loaded (refer to Figure 14-1)

+ **Hardware**: Shows your PlayBook PIN, storage and memory breakdown, and when you last booted

+ **OS**: Shows you the OS version and build ID, Flash player version, Adobe Air version, and kernel version

+ **Network**: Shows details about the specific network that you are con-nected to, including IPv6 and IPv4 address and your MAC address

+ **Legal**: Shows some information about third-party software and a hyperlink to the full license and copyright information for the PlayBook

Managing Bluetooth Connections

Although the BlackBerry Bridge connection to your BlackBerry smartphone is made through a Bluetooth wireless connection, the Bluetooth 2.1+ radio installed on your PlayBook has other uses. As of June 2011, RIM provided these four Bluetooth profiles:

+ **Dial-up Networking (DUN)**: Provides Internet access through a paired mobile phone. Your PlayBook does not need a wireless carrier data plan and can piggyback onto your mobile phone network access.

+ **Serial Port Profile (SPP)**: Emulates a serial cable and provides a sub-stitute for RS-232. This is actually the profile that connects your BlackBerry smartphone using BlackBerry Bridge.

+ **Secure Simply Pairing (SSP)**: A feature of the 2.1+ specification; that improves the pairing experience (discussed next) while increasing the strength of security.

+ **Human Interface Device (HID)**: Provides support for control devices such as Bluetooth keyboards.

MISSING BLUETOOTH PROFILES You may notice that stereo headphone (A2DP) and headset (HSP) profiles are missing from the PlayBook Bluetooth profiles. Unfortunately, this means you cannot use a pair of Bluetooth headphones to enjoy audio content on your PlayBook, but RIM promises to provide these profiles in a future update.

To set up a Bluetooth connection with a mobile phone, follow these steps:

1. From the Settings page tap the Bluetooth setting found near the top of the left column. The Bluetooth management page appears, as shown in Figure 14-2.

FIGURE 14-2 Bluetooth connections page

2. Swipe the toggle to the On position.

3. Ensure the mobile phone or device you want to pair with has Bluetooth turned on, is visible, and is in discoverable mode.

4. Tap the Add New Device button in the bottom right. A new device display appears, as shown in Figure 14-3.

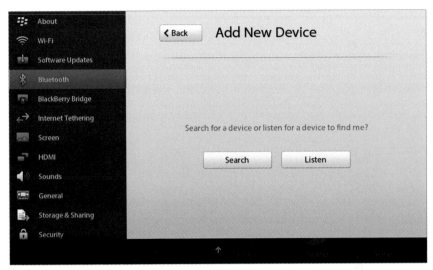

FIGURE 14-3 Adding a new Bluetooth device

5. Tap the Listen button for your PlayBook to listen for devices scanning for a connection or tap the Search button to search for discoverable devices that are not actively scanning. Devices found are listed on your PlayBook.

6. Tap a device you want to pair with. A pairing number and instructions appear, as shown in Figure 14-4. Verify that the number on your PlayBook matches the number on your phone, which is a function of that SSP profile mentioned earlier, and tap Yes if they do match. Your paired phone then appears on your main Bluetooth page to be used for tethering purposes, as detailed later in this chapter.

- -

CAN I PAIR ANOTHER BLUETOOTH DEVICE? You can use this same process to pair your PlayBook with other devices, such as Bluetooth keyboards. Your PlayBook walks you through the process with directions and prompts to assist you.

- -

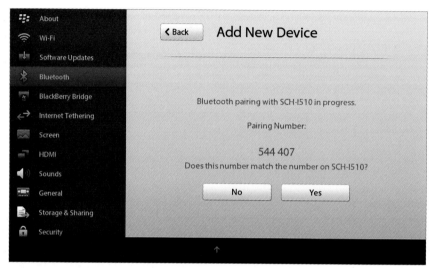

FIGURE 14-4 Actively pairing with a new phone

For security reasons, you should turn off the discoverability of your PlayBook using the Discoverable drop-down. Choices include On, Off, and Off After 2 Minutes. You can also remove a paired device by tapping the Edit button (a Pencil icon) and then tapping the Delete button (Trash Can icon), as shown in Figure 14-5. There is no confirmation of deletion, so after you tap the Trash Can icon the device will be removed, but it is easy to add it back later. If you tap a device name in your list of paired devices, you can view the properties of that device.

FIGURE 14-5 Removing a device from the list of paired devices

Setting Up Internet Tethering

The process to connect your PlayBook to a BlackBerry smartphone was discussed in detail in Chapter 5 (How Do I Bridge the PlayBook with My BlackBerry Smartphone?), but you may have another type of smartphone and want to tether your PlayBook to it so that you can connect to the Internet. Use the Internet tethering setting to connect to the Internet via a Bluetooth wireless connection.

CAN I CONNECT TO MY PHONE VIA WI-FI INSTEAD OF BLUETOOTH?
Many smartphones today have integrated Wi-Fi hotspots. Using that method of tethering is handled in the same manner as connecting your PlayBook to other Wi-Fi hotspots.

To connect your PlayBook to the Internet through a mobile phone that is not a BlackBerry, follow these steps:

1. Pair your mobile phone to your PlayBook, as detailed in the previous section of this chapter.

2. In the Settings area, tap the words Internet Tethering in the left column. The Internet tethering page opens with your paired device in the list, as shown in Figure 14-6.

FIGURE 14-6 Internet tethering page

3. Tap the phone you want to set up for tethering with your PlayBook. A page to manage your phone settings appears, as shown in Figure 14-7.

FIGURE 14-7 Setting up your phone to tether

4. From the list of wireless service providers, tap the one associated with your mobile phone. Because the list of carriers is extensive, you can enter your carrier name in the search box to find it faster. A page for your carrier appears with some carrier profiles requiring more information.

5. Tap the Connect button on your carrier profile page, as shown in Figure 14-8. You may see a warning about tethering charges, so make sure you understand the tethering policies of your carrier and your plan. Tap the Continue button on this warning page.

WHAT IF MY CARRIER ISN'T LISTED? You can manually add a wireless service profile by tapping the Add Profile button. You then enter the profile name, access point, username, and password, if applicable, and tap the Connect button to make your connection (see Figure 14-9).

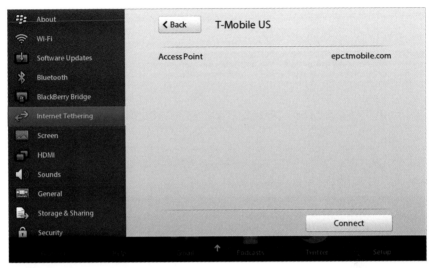

FIGURE 14-8 Carrier profile page

FIGURE 14-9 Internet tethering page

6. You then see some connection status notes and are taken back to the main Internet tethering page where you see your device connection status and time length of connection, as shown in Figure 14-10. You can now use your PlayBook to connect to the Internet through your mobile phone connection.

FIGURE 14-10   Internet tethering page showing an active connection

CHECK OUT THE HOME SCREEN STATUS POP-UP   You can quickly check the connection status by simply tapping the Bluetooth icon from your Home screen upper Status bar. A pop-up appears, as shown in Figure 14-11, where you can easily disconnect from your phone and turn off the Bluetooth radio.

FIGURE 14-11   Home screen connection status management

To disconnect the tethered phone, visit the Internet tethering settings, and tap on the large Disconnect button centered at the bottom of the display.

Controlling Screen Time-Out and Brightness

The BlackBerry PlayBook's high-resolution LCD display is bright and brilliant, and this can impact the battery life if you keep it at maximum brightness all the time. You can adjust your display in the screen settings area. To do so, perform the following:

1. From the Settings page, tap the Screen setting found near the middle of the left column, and the screen management page appears (see Figure 14-12). You see two main buttons: one for battery settings and one for plugged in settings. Both have the four following options:

FIGURE 14-12 Screen management page

- **Brightness**: Slide the marker or tap the slider bar to adjust the display brightness to your liking. You can also adjust the brightness to turn the automatic backlight dimming on or off.
- **Backlight time-out**: Use the drop-down selector to choose from 10 seconds to 5 minutes for when the backlight on the display will go

out. When the backlight goes out, the screen auto-dims down to the lowest level but is still readable in low-light conditions. To turn the backlight on, simply tap or swipe the display.

✛ **Automatic backlight dimming**: Slide this On to enable your light sensor to pick up ambient light and automatically control the backlight, which should give you an optimal viewing experience and decent battery life.

✛ **Standby time-out**: Use the drop-down selector to choose from 30 seconds to 5 minutes. When the time-out kicks in, you need to perform a swipe gesture from the frame toward the center of the display to "wake" your device back up.

2. Select the four options for your battery power, and then tap the plugged-in button to do the same for when your device is plugged in. By default, the plugged-in modes are all set to maximum brightness and time-out limits, given that you have a constant source of power.

The display settings you make with the slider bar and selectors take effect as soon as you make a selection. There is no save or restart required to apply your settings.

Setting the HDMI Preferences

One functionality that helps your PlayBook serve as a media hub for sharing with others is the HDMI out support. You can manage these options for when you connect to a TV or external monitor by navigating to the Settings page and tapping the HDMI setting found toward the middle of the left column. The HDMI management page appears, as shown in Figure 14-13. Here you can see five options for managing your HDMI preferences:

✛ **Default to Mirror Mode**: In mirror mode your external monitor shows exactly what is on your PlayBook display at all times. If you turn off mirror mode, you only see something on your external display when the application supports HDMI out in presenter mode. Presenter mode is supported in Slideshow To Go and Videos.

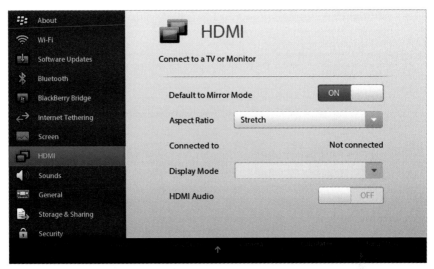

FIGURE 14-13 HDMI preferences page

+ **Aspect Ratio**: This option is only available if you have mirror mode turned on; if you do, you can select from the following:

  + **Normal (1:1)**: Shows the PlayBook display as it appears in your hand and is the preferred mode.
  + **Stretch**: Stretches your display to fit as best as possible.
  + **Zoom**: Zooms in to some undefined level to see objects appear a bit bigger.
  + **Fill**: Intended to fill the external display with your PlayBook display, but in my experience it exceeded the external display borders.

+ **Connected To**: This line simply tells you the name of the external monitor or TV to which you are connected.

+ **Display Mode**: After you make an HDMI connection, you have the option to switch between one of 12 different resolutions and frequencies. The default preferred selection is 1280x720p@60Hz[16:9], but you can choose from any other one and immediately see the result on your display.

➕ **HDMI Audio Toggle**: Turn this on to hear the audio from your PlayBook through the HDMI port from the speakers of your selected TV or external monitor. By default, this toggle is turned on when you connect an HDMI cable.

As you can see in Figure 14-14, the last three settings require that you have your PlayBook connected via HDMI to your external display.

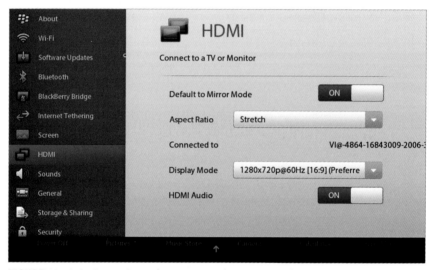

FIGURE 14-14 Active settings when connected to an external monitor

Managing Your PlayBook Sounds

The Sounds Settings page is found near the bottom of your left settings list and, as shown in Figure 14-15, provides preferences to manage the volume levels for three functions:

➕ **Master Volume**: Controls the volume level of the entire device. This volume level can be managed with the slider here or more commonly through the volume buttons on the top of your PlayBook.

➕ **Keyboard Feedback**: You can control the volume level of the acknowledgment when you tap on the virtual keyboard with this setting.

➕ **Notifications**: This slider bar controls the volume for notifications that come from received messages, calendar appointments, and tasks that are due.

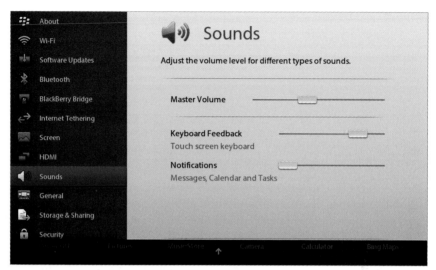

FIGURE 14-15 Sounds management page

TYPICAL SOUND PLAYED FOR YOU TO TEST As you slide or tap along the selection bar, the sound is activated at that level, so you can easily adjust and select just the volume level that you want.

Selecting the General Background Application Settings

As you know by now, your PlayBook is a multitasking wonder, and jumping from one open application to another is a breeze. The general settings enable you to manage application behavior and turn on demo mode if you want to set up your PlayBook to show some functionality to others. To do so follow these steps:

1. From the Settings page tap the General setting found near the bottom of the left column, and the General preferences page appears, as shown in Figure 14-16.

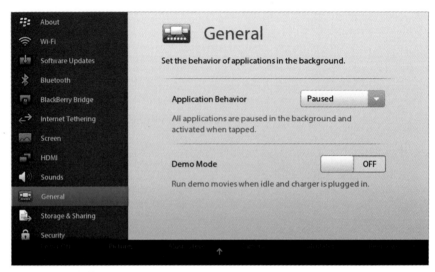

FIGURE 14-16 General Settings page

2. Tap the drop-down selector next to Application Behavior to choose from one of these three options:

+ **Showcase**: All open applications are active and never pause in the background.

+ **Default**: An application stays active in the background until another application goes full screen. This explains why you can see video running in a minimized window until you open up another application.

+ **Paused**: See all applications pause in the background and activate only when tapped.

3. Tap the demo mode toggle to turn it on if you want to see the demo movies run on your PlayBook when it is plugged in and idle.

The different application behavior choices can impact battery life, so choose only what you know meets your needs and try not to have all applications actively running in the background at all times.

Managing Your Storage and Sharing Preferences

When you connect your PlayBook via USB or Wi-Fi to your computer, you have different options to handle the communication method. The Storage and Sharing options enable you to preselect the default behavior for these connections. Chapter 10 (How Can I View, Share, and Capture Pictures on My PlayBook?), provides the details of how to make a successful Wi-Fi connection for transferring photos and covers most of the settings on the Storage and Sharing page. A couple of Storage and Sharing security settings were not mentioned there, however; these include the USB Connections option and the File Sharing toggle. To manage USB Connections settings (see Figure 14-17), complete the following:

1. From the Settings page tap the Storage and Sharing setting found near the bottom of the left column.

2. Tap the drop-down arrow next to the first option, USB Connections.

3. Choose from three options:

    + Automatically Detect

    + Connect to Windows

    + Connect to Mac

FIGURE 14-17 Storage & Sharing options for USB connections

To manage File Sharing settings, complete the following:

1. From the Settings page tap the Storage and Sharing setting found near the bottom of the left column.

2. Tap the toggle next to the File Sharing option to turn it on. This will allow access and sharing of your tablet's file and media over a USB connection, as shown in Figure 14-18. If you do not want to share anything, you can turn it off and help keep your PlayBook secure.

FIGURE 14-18 File sharing via USB toggle is on.

Related Questions

+ Where else can I find some diagnostic information on my PlayBook?
  PAGE 21

+ Can I play Power Point presentations via HDMI? **PAGE 139**

+ Where can I choose what sound to have for an alarm? **PAGE 214**

CHAPTER FIFTEEN

HOW DO I MANAGE MY PLAYBOOK WITH BLACKBERRY DESKTOP SOFTWARE?

In this chapter:

+ Installing BlackBerry Desktop
+ Desktop Options
+ Device Options
+ Manage Media Sync
+ Back Up Options
+ Switch and Forget Devices

Y ou can set up and use your BlackBerry PlayBook without any kind of desk-top or bridged smartphone connection, but your experience can improve remarkably if you download, install, and use the BlackBerry Desktop Software for the PlayBook. With this additional software, you can sync your existing media to your PlayBook via the desktop software; back up your PlayBook; update your PlayBook's software; and use it to help you switch devices. Support for the PlayBook is currently provided for Windows PCs; Mac support is coming in a future update.

Installing BlackBerry Desktop

The last part of the Setup Wizard, described in detail in Chapter 2 (How Do I Set Up and Customize My PlayBook?) shows an icon for BlackBerry Desktop Software. To install your BlackBerry Desktop software, start from here and follow these steps:

1. From your Windows computer enter this link (`www.blackberry.com/DesktopSoftware`) and select download. An Installation Wizard appears to walk you through installing the software. RIM plans to release a Mac version of the Desktop Software in late 2011.

2. After you finish installing the software, launch it to set up your PlayBook connection.

3. A status screen appears on both your PlayBook (see Figure 15-1) and on your Windows PC (see Figure 15-2) to help you get your PlayBook con-nected. Here you can edit your device name, select what to do when you make your connection, and view what media will sync to your device if you choose to do so, as shown in Figure 15-3.

The user interface is fairly basic (see Figure 15-4); two main menus are in the upper left for Device and Tools. Some buttons display in the left column for music, pictures, and videos with a status screen in the middle of the dis-play. Before you can start syncing content, you need to make sure the options in these menus are at the proper setting.

FIGURE 15-1 Connected status screen on the PlayBook

FIGURE 15-2 Confirmation that you have successfully connected to your PC

FIGURE 15-3 Name your PlayBook and select your settings.

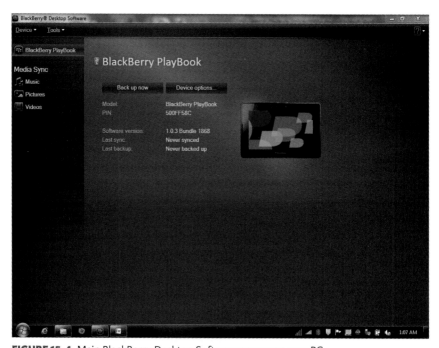

FIGURE 15-4 Main BlackBerry Desktop Software screen on your PC

Desktop Options

Before you can start syncing content between your PC and PlayBook, you need to make some choices and set up the program for your specific needs and desires. To do so, follow these steps:

1. From the top-left area, click Tools; then select the Desktop options.

2. A display with two tabs, as shown in Figure 15-5 and 15-6, appears with several options. The software is regularly updated and you may see slightly different options with the latest software version. Read through them and choose the settings you desire.

3. After making your selections, tap the OK button to apply these settings to your setup so that you can proceed to device options.

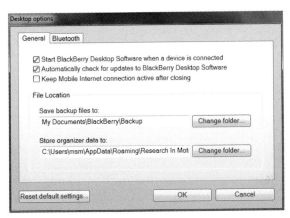

FIGURE 15-5 General desktop options

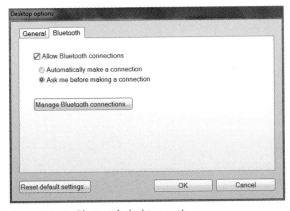

FIGURE 15-6 Bluetooth desktop options

Device Options

Now that the PC side of the equation is set up, you can set up your device-specific options.

1. In the top left, click the Device menu; then choose Device Options from the list.

2. A page of device options appears with three tabs: General, Media, and Backup, as shown in Figure 15-7.

FIGURE 15-7 General device options screen on your PC

3. Look through the available options on the General tab and make your selections. Options for you to select from on the General tab include the following:

   + **Device Name**: By default your device name appears here, but you can change it and it will be reflected on your device.

   + **Back up my device**: Toggle on and you can use the drop-down to choose from daily, weekly, biweekly, and monthly.

+ **Media files**: Toggle on to choose to sync media files.

+ **Notify me:** Toggle and email address field for notification of future updates.

ITUNES SUPPORTS ALBUM ART The BlackBerry PlayBook Desktop Software is more feature-packed if you use iTunes rather than Windows Media Player due to things such as album art support in iTunes.

---

4. Click the Media tab to choose from the following options, as shown in Figure 15-8:

+ **Music source:** Choose iTunes or Windows Media Player.

+ **Media location:** Designate where to store pictures and videos.

+ **Media on My Device:** Select settings to view and manage media on your device.

FIGURE 15-8 Device options Media tab

5. Click the final tab to manage your backup settings (see Figure 15-9). These settings include:

✛ **Skip confirmations on**: Choose when you want to see skip confirmations: manual or automatic backups.

✛ **Preferred Backup Settings**: Choose between Full (all device data and settings) and Custom (selected data only) and click the box on the multitude of available data options.

✛ **Backup Files:** Designate where backup files get saved and toggle to encrypt your data backup file.

FIGURE 15-9 Device backup settings

Manage Media Sync

With your desktop and PlayBook settings now enabled and customized, you can set up the details of your music, pictures, and videos sync. To do so, follow these steps:

1. Tap the left-column menu, labeled Media Sync, and note Music, Pictures, and Videos in that column.

2. Select the Music option to see your music collection categorized by artist, playlist, and genre, as shown in Figure 15-10. Select exactly what you want by clicking the boxes; then they sync to your PlayBook.

3. Tap the Pictures and Videos lines in the column to see pages with two tabs: one for your device and one for your computer, as shown in Figure 15-11.

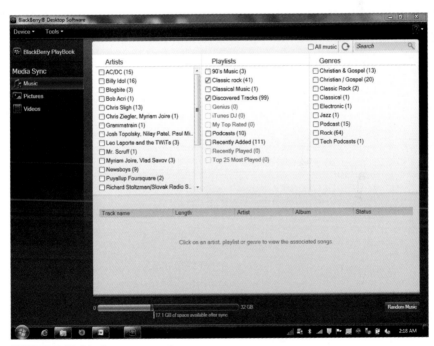

FIGURE 15-10 Music management page

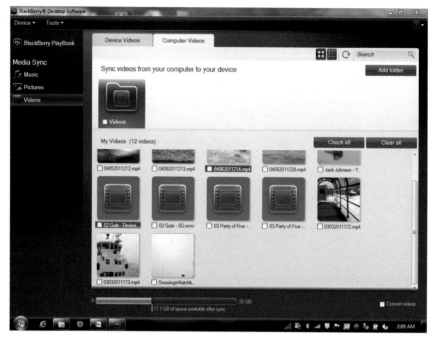

FIGURE 15-11 Videos management page

Back Up Options

The first time you connect your PlayBook to your PC, you see a Back Up Options page, as shown Figure 15-12. This Back Up Options page is similar to the backup settings for the new PlayBook. All the same fields are present, with the addition of an option to encrypt the backup and enter passwords. After making your selections and choosing some data to back up, click the Back up button to apply the changes and start the backup. When you actually back up your device, a status screen appears similar to what you see in Figure 15-13. A confirmation page appears when the backup is completed.

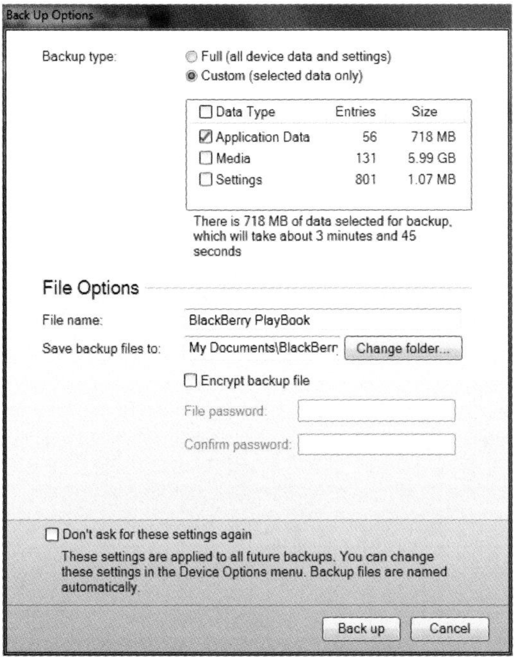

FIGURE 15-12 Device options media tab

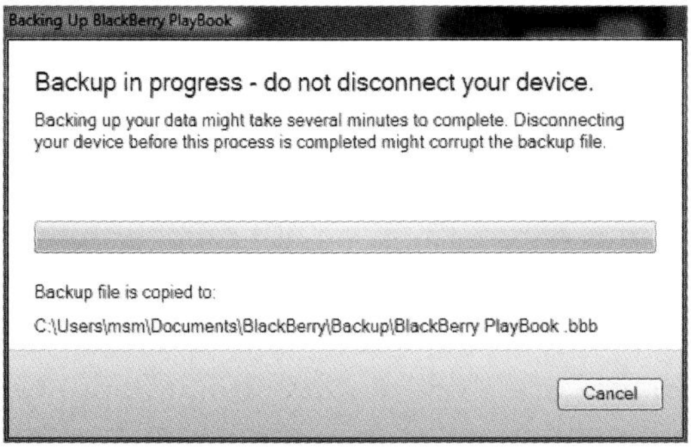

FIGURE 15-13 Back up your PlayBook

Switch and Forget Devices

RIM makes it easy for you to switch to a new device or remove selected devices from your PC. In the top-left, click the Device menu to find both Switch Devices and Forget Device (see Figure 15-14). If you select to switch a device, you are prompted to connect your current device so that files can be copied to your PC for later copying onto a new device.

FIGURE 15-14 Switch and forget devices menu items

 If you want to remove a device from your list of devices, simply select the Forget Device option to have it removed.

Related Questions

   ✦ Can I check for software updates from my PlayBook? **PAGE 29**

   ✦ Where can I find music to put on my PlayBook? **PAGE 146**

   ✦ How can I wipe a device clean? **PAGE 252**

CHAPTER SIXTEEN

HOW DO I TROUBLESHOOT MY PLAYBOOK?

In this chapter:

+ General Techniques for Troubleshooting

+ BlackBerry Bridge Issues

+ Browser Issues

+ Wi-Fi Connection Issues

+ Bluetooth Device Connection Issues

+ HDMI Issues

A s hard as RIM worked on the PlayBook, nothing is perfect, and you may run into an issue every once in a while. Because the PlayBook runs a new mobile operating system, it is common for the problem you experience to stem from simple human error, but there are also the rare hardware or software glitches. The good news is that a majority of these issues can be solved quickly and easily by you without having to take or send the device in to the manufacturer.

General Techniques for Troubleshooting

Before you visit your local electronics store or send your device to RIM for repairs, check through these different techniques to see if your particular issue can be fixed.

RESTART YOUR PLAYBOOK

The easiest thing to try first if your PlayBook acts up is to turn it off and then on again. Additionally, you can try restarting your phone if you have one paired with your PlayBook, which also clears out the running processes. To restart your PlayBook, simply press and hold the Power button for a couple of seconds; then tap Restart when it appears.

NO BATTERY REMOVAL OPTION ON THE PLAYBOOK You may pop out the battery on your smartphone to fix issues sometimes, but remember that there is no removable battery on the PlayBook so that is not an option—there is no need to pry the case apart.

RECHARGE YOUR PLAYBOOK

Although the PlayBook does have a long lasting battery, it is possible that the problem you experience is simply due to a battery that is completely drained. The BlackBerry PlayBook has a standard microUSB port to charge your device, so you can connect to a computer or A/C charger to give your tablet some juice. Unfortunately, there is no battery indicator light, so the only way to check the charging Status is to turn the device on and tap on the Battery icon in the upper Status bar.

20% BATTERY LEVEL IS REQUIRED Your PlayBook will not allow you to complete the update process if you have less than 20% battery life remaining. Even if you have your PlayBook plugged in to charge, you will be unable to install an update until the battery reaches at least a 20% level.

BACK TO THE HOME SCREEN AND TRY AGAIN

If you run an application and it locks up, try swiping up from the bottom frame to go back to the Home screen and relaunch the application. The PlayBook has a limited amount of RAM to run programs, so if you run several apps, you may need to quit a few to free up some available memory. Remember that you can simply tap the app in the Home screen selector and swipe it up and off the display to close it.

CHECK FOR A PLAYBOOK UPDATE

Your PlayBook automatically informs you when there is a software update via a notification on the screen, so you should know about available updates. However, if your device appears to be acting up, you may want to manually check for an update that could resolve the issue you have. To manually check for an update, follow these steps:

1. Tap the Gear icon in the upper right of the Home screen, or swipe down from the top frame on the Home screen to access the settings area.

2. Tap on Software Updates from the left column of settings.

3. Tap the Check for Updates button to check for a PlayBook update (see Figure 16-1).

4. If there is an update available, it displays on this screen. Follow the specific directions given to install the update. If you are up-to-date, the PlayBook lets you know.

FIGURE 16-1 Tap to check for updates.

CHECK FOR APP UPDATES

Applications are updated from time to time with improved performance, new features, or for other reasons. If you have an application issue, follow these steps to check for an update:

1. Tap the BlackBerry App World icon from your Home screen to launch App World.

2. Look at the My World tab in the top-left corner of your display. Your PlayBook automatically shows when application updates are available for your installed apps with a red asterisk on the words My World (see Figure 16-2).

3. Tap the My World tab, and swipe up and down in your list of installed apps to view what app(s) have updates (see Figure 16-3).

4. Tap the Upgrade button to download and install the application update.

FIGURE 16-2 Updates shown as available with red asterisk

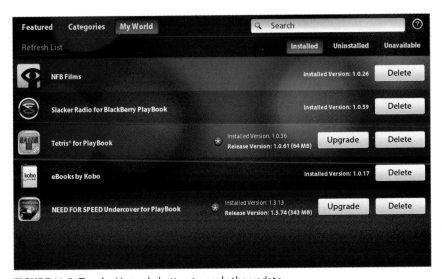

FIGURE 16-3 Tap the Upgrade button to apply the update.

WIPE YOUR PLAYBOOK

If none of the techniques previously mentioned solve your issue, one of the first things a technical support customer service representative will tell you on the phone to do is to reset your device. Chapter 13 (How Do I Keep My PlayBook Secure?) describes how to perform a security wipe of your PlayBook. Keep in mind that performing this security wipe can take your device back to factory condition and require that you set it up and reinstall any applications you loaded onto your PlayBook.

BlackBerry Bridge Issues

As discussed in detail in Chapter 5 (How Do I Bridge the PlayBook with My BlackBerry Smartphone?) you can connect your PlayBook via Bluetooth to access your email messages, calendar, contacts, files, web browser, and BlackBerry Messenger. If you have issues with this connection, check the following things:

+ **Active Bluetooth connection on both devices**: Check to make sure that the Bluetooth radio is turned on for both your PlayBook and BlackBerry smartphone and that the two are paired together.

+ **Updated BlackBerry Bridge software installed on your smartphone**: Visit BlackBerry App World on your smartphone to see if the Bridge software is up-to-date.

+ **Updated version of BBM installed on your smartphone**: Even if the Bridge software is updated, make sure other software that works through the Bridge connection is also updated. Again, visit BlackBerry App World on your smartphone to check for software updates.

+ **Reconnect your smartphone via the BlackBerry Bridge**: As detailed in Chapter 5, visit the BlackBerry Bridge settings on your PlayBook to try to set up the connection with your phone again.

CONNECTION MAY JUST BE TIMED OUT If you move your PlayBook away from your BlackBerry smartphone or some other event causes the active connection to break, it may appear that you are no longer bridged because the Bridge app icons appear with yellow exclamation marks, as shown in Figure 16-4. After you move into range and ensure Bluetooth is active on both devices, tap a Bridge application and the connection should activate again.

FIGURE 16-4 No smartphone is connected to these Bridge apps.

Browser Issues

The PlayBook web browser is one of the most powerful parts of the PlayBook experience and for the most part should give you a near desktop experience. Make sure you have an active data connection when using the web browser. If you do experience issues while browsing, check that the media format you are viewing is supported by the PlayBook.

I CAN ONLY SEE PARTS OF A WEBSITE Some websites may attempt to categorize the PlayBook browser as a mobile device and present you with a limited browsing experience. If this occurs, look around on the web page for an option to select the full version of the website to view on your PlayBook.

Wi-Fi Connection Issues

Success of the 802.11 b/g/n Wi-Fi connection made from your PlayBook is dependent on the router providing the wireless signal that connects to the Internet. If a problem occurs and you suspect it may relate to Wi-Fi connection, try the following:

1. First check the router providing the signal. Try using another device or your PC to test the Wi-Fi connection to verify it is indeed working properly.

2. After you determine that the Wi-Fi access point is set up and working properly, check to make sure you actually have the Wi-Fi radio enabled on your PlayBook. As detailed in Chapter 2 (How Do I Set Up and Customize My PlayBook?), this is found in the Wi-Fi settings and in your upper Status bar.

3. If you connect to a secured network, double-check that the password was entered correctly. RIM enables you to show the password on your PlayBook display as you enter it to help ensure you have entered it correctly.

Bluetooth Device Connection Issues

A Bluetooth connection is used primarily to connect to your smartphone for BlackBerry Bridge functions but can also be used for Internet tethering, keyboard connections, and more. If you have Bluetooth connection issues, first check that the Bluetooth radio is enabled on both devices and that they have been paired. As detailed in Chapter 14 (How Do I Manage Settings on My

PlayBook?) you can always remove a device from your Bluetooth connection list and reconnect if you have problems.

HDMI Issues

HDMI output can be useful for enjoying media on a large screen or giving presentations to your audience with your PlayBook. If you have issues with HDMI output, you can check a couple of things:

+ **Check HDMI settings**: Make sure to review Chapter 14 and ensure your HDMI mode settings are what you need for your current session.

+ **Check the cable**: The most common issue with HDMI output is the cable connection between your PlayBook and the cable and the cable and your external display. Even though this is a simple check, it is often the one that people forget about, so check those cable connections.

Related Questions

+ How can I return to my Home screen and view the upper Status bar? **PAGE 41**

+ How can I get movies on my PlayBook to use HDMI? **PAGE 169**

+ Where can I check out my settings? **PAGE 258**

+ INDEX

Numbers

7digital music store
  browsing, 154–156
  menu, 50–52
  purchasing music, 155–156

A

About Page, 258–259
Adobe Reader, 236–238
  security settings, 241
Album art history (Music app), 153
album art in iTunes, 281
aligning text, 127, 133
Amazon Cloud Player, 160
Android app player, 12
API (application programming interface),
  buttons and, 6
app players, 12
App World, 35, 216–219
Apple iPad, 14
Application View, gestures, 41
applications
  gestures, 43
  icons, 46
  minimized, 45–46
Applications Behavior, 272
appointments (Calendar), creating,
  107–108
apps (applications)
  Bing Maps, 200–203
  browsing for, 216–219
  Calculator, 208–213
  Clock, 213
    alarm, 214–215
    stopwatch, 215
    timer, 215
  copies, 36

default, 35–36
downloading, 219–222
games
  Need for Speed Undercover,
    204–205
  Tetris, 205–208
installation, 219–222
moving, 36
multiple, 53
Music, 146
permissions, 240–244
preloaded, 198–216
searching for, 216–219
switching between, 52–54
unavailable, 222
unstalling, 36–37
updates, 290–291
Weather, 198–200
weather, menu, 51
aspect ratio, 269
audio
  music formats, 147
  stereo speakers, 4
audio toggle (HDMI), 270

B

Back Up Options, 284–285
backlight
  automatic dimming, 268
  time-out, 267–268
backup settings, 282
battery
  charging contacts, 8
  display resolution and, 267
  indicator, 49
  recharge in troubleshooting, 288–289
  removing in troubleshooting, 288

BBM (BlackBerry Messenger)
  Bridge and, 84–88
  chat, 85
  profile, 87
  search, 86
Bing Maps, 200–203
BlackBerry App World, 216–219
BlackBerry Bridge
  setup, 29–32
    Bluetooth, 78–80
  setup screen, 79
  toggle, 48
  troubleshooting, 292–293
BlackBerry Desktop software
  Desktop options, 279
  Device Options, 280–282
  installation, 276–278
  music transfer, 148–149
BlackBerry ID
  agreement, 27
  setup, 27–28
BlackBerry Rapid Charging Pad, 8
Bluetooth
  A2DP (stereo headphone), 260
  Bridge setup, 78–80
  connection indicator, 49
  connection setup, 260–262
  discoverability, 262
  DUN (dial-up networking), 259
  HID (human interface device), 259
  HSP (headset), 260
  pairing devices, 260–262
  photo transfer, 178
  SPP (serial port profile), 259
  SSP (secure simply pairing), 259
  troubleshooting connection, 294–295
bold text, 126
bookmarks
  adding, 73
  Bridge Browser, 84
  documents, 127
  Gold Star, 73
  Star with Green Plus, 73
box contents, 10
Bridge Browser, 60, 82
  auto start, 88
  BBM (BlackBerry Messenger), 84–88

  bookmarks, 84
  email, 90–97
    attachments, 95
    composing new, 96–97
    controls, 92
    filter by account, 90
    portrait orientation, 94
    searches, 95
  Facebook, 90
  favorites tab, 83
  shortcuts, 83
  speed, 83
  Twitter, 90
Bridge Files, 80–81
  opening, 81–82
brightness of display, 267
browser, troubleshooting, 293–294
browsing Web for apps, 216–219. *See also*
  Web browsing
buttons
  documents, 126–127
  media control, 6
  Play/Pause, 6
  Power button, 6
  Volume, 6

C

cache clearing, 71
Calculator
  scientific mode, 209
  standard mode, 208–209
  Tip Calculator, 212–213
  unit converter, 210–212
Calendar, 102
  appointments, creating, 107–108
  filtering services, 104–105
  navigating, 104
  service colors, 105
  sources, 104
  Tungle, 105
  views, 102–103
calendar icon, 46
camera
  forward facing, 5
  rear facing, 9

Camera app
    capturing picture, 188–191
        options, 189
    front-facing camera, 190
    ratio, 190
    stabilizing images, 190
    video recording, 165–167
Caps Lock, 55
capturing photos, 188–191
capturing screenshots, 193
categories of tabs, 35
certificates, 244–246
charging, contacts, 8
chat. *See also* Video Chat
    BBM (BlackBerry Messenger), 85
check box icon, 46
Clock app, 213
closing apps, gestures, 42
Cloud Player (Amazon), 160
computer
    connecting to, 185
    PlayBook as external drive, 148
Contacts
    creating, 110–112
    deleting, 110
    editing, 110
    links, 112
    Video Chat, 172
    viewing, 109–110
Content options for web browser, 68–69
cookies, 70
    clearing, 72
.csv files, 132
customizing wallpaper, 34–35

D

data linking spreadsheets, 138
Date and Time setup, 26
Desktop options (Desktop software), 279
Desktop software, music transfer, 148–149
development environments, 11–12
development mode, 246
    enabling, 247–248
Device options (Desktop software),
    280–282

devices
    forget device, 286
    switch devices, 286
display, 4
    backlight
        automatic dimming, 268
        time-out, 267–268
    brightness, 267
    gesture, 41
    HDMI and, 269
    HDMI port, 8
    Power button, 6
    resolution, battery life and, 267
    standby time-out, 268
documents
    bold text, 126
    bookmarks, 127
    button controls, 126–127
    format, 131
    italic text, 126
    saving, 130–131
    underline text, 126
    word count, 127
    Word To Go
        creating, 125–131
        editing, 128–130
        transferring, 124
        viewing, 122–125
Documents To Go, 122
    save location, 81
    Sheet To Go, 131
        clearing cells, 136
        creating spreadsheets, 133–136
        data linking, 138
        editing spreadsheets, 136–137
        formulas, 137
        hiding cells, 136
        number styles, 134
        showing cells, 136
        text manipulation, 138
        transferring spreadsheets, 132
        viewing spreadsheet, 132
    Slideshow To Go, 139
        PlayBook presentations, 142
        presentation viewing, 140–141
        rearranging slideshow, 141

Word To Go
    creating documents, 125–131
    editing documents, 128–130
    saving documents, 130–131
    transferring document, 124
    viewing document, 122
downloads, 75
    apps, 219–222
    podcasts, 162–164
dragging, 45

E

eBooks
    Adobe Reader, 236–238
    EPUB, 224
    Kobo eReader
        buying eBooks, 224–229
        reading books, 230–236
email
    Bridge, 90–97
        attachments, 95
        composing new, 96–97
        controls, 92
        filter by account, 90
        portrait orientation, 94
        searches, 95
    icons, 98
    photo sharing, 194
    standalone applications, 100
    web browser, 97–98
        Gmail view, 98
envelope icon, 46
EPUB eBooks, 224
exclamation point icon, 46
external drive, PlayBook as, 148
external storage, 178

F

Facebook
    Bridge, 90
    security settings, 241
File Sharing settings, 274
files
    Bridge, 80–81
    .csv, 132
    transferring, limits, 124–125

filtering email, Bridge, 90
fonts, 127
    spreadsheets, 133
forget device, 286
formatting text, 126–127
forward facing camera, 5, 190

G

Galaxy Tab, 16–17
games
    Need for Speed Undercover, 204–205
    Tetris, 205–208
Gear icon, 49
General preferences page, 271–272
    Application Behavior, 272
General settings for web browser, 67–68
gestures
    dragging, 45
    pinching, 45
    swipe, 41–43
    tapping, 43
    touch and hold, 44
Gmail email view, 98
Gold Star, bookmarks and, 73

H

hardware, About Page, 259
HD TV, 8
HDMI
    aspect ratio, 269
    audio toggle, 270
    connections, 269
    display mode, 269
    mirror mode default, 268
    photo sharing, 195
    troubleshooting, 295
    video watching, 169
HDMI port, 8
headset jack, 6, 7
Home screen, 40
    About Page, 258–259
    applications
        icons, 46
        minimized, 45–46
    gestures, 41
    icon, 75

notifications, exclamation point icon, 46
notifications area, 45
returning to in troubleshooting, 289
shortcuts, Bridge Browser, 83
Status bar, 45
hotspots. *See* Wi-Fi
HTTP Proxy, Wi-Fi network, 23
hyperlinks, 62

I

icons
applications, 46
email, 98
Gear, 49
moving, 44
pulsing, 36
Status bar, 48
Tasks, 113
images
Bridge Files, 81
wallpaper, 34
indenting text, 127
initial startup, 20–21
BlackBerry ID, 27–28
Date and Time, 26
Wi-Fi connection, 21–26
installation
apps, 219–222
BlackBerry Desktop software, 276–278
IP address, 185
Mac connection, 187
Windows connection, 185–186
iPad, 14
italic text, 126
iTunes album art, 281

J

Java SDK and app player, 12
justified text alignment, 133

K

keyboard, 54–56
feedback, 270
gestures, 42

Kobo eReader
buying eBooks, 224–229
reading eBooks, 230–236

L

labeling, 8
landscape orientation in Word To Go, 123
launching applications, gestures, 43
LED indicator/light sensor, 4
legal information About Page, 259
linking spreadsheets, 138
links, Contacts, 112
local storage, clearing, 72

M

Macintosh
IP address, 187
USB photo sharing, 182–183
maps, Bing Maps, 200–203
media control buttons, 6
Media Player, 153
Media Sync, 283–284
music sync, 148–149
memory card, photo transfer, 178
Memos, 115–116
menus
gestures, 42
weather application, 51
web browser, 50
messages
BBM (BlackBerry Messenger), 84
notifications, 47
micro USB port, 8
microkernel architecture, 11
microphones, 6–7
minimized applications, 45–46
mirror mode, 268
monitor, display output to, 8
Motorola Xoom, 14–15
music
Amazon Cloud Player, 160
Bridge Files, 81
controlling, 151–154
formats, 147
Media Sync and, 148–149
purchasing, 155–156

Slacker Radio, 156–159
transferring to PlayBook, 147–148
BlackBerry Desktop software,
148–149
Music app, 146
controls, 152–153
playing music, 152
playlists
adding, 149–150
removing, 150
music controller indicator, 48
mute toggling, 7

N

NDK (Native Development Kit), 11
Need for Speed Undercover game,
204–205
networks
About Page, 259
Wi-Fi
connecting to, 21–26
listed, 23–24
notifications
calendar icon, 46
check box icon, 46
envelope icon, 46
exclamation point icon, 46
messages, 47
notifications area, 45
red glow, 47
Sounds Settings, 270
number styles in spreadsheets, 134

O

operating system, QNX Neutrino, 11
options, gestures, 44
orientation, portrait, 49
orientation lock indicator, 48
OS (operating system), About Page, 259

P

pairing Bluetooth devices, 260–262
panning, gestures, 42

paragraph formatting, 127
password
changing, 251
forgotten, 251
remembering, 187
resetting, 28
setting, 249–251
PDF To Go, 142–144
Pencil button, 65
permissions
applications, 240–244
web browser, 69–70
photos
albums, thumbnails, 192
capturing, 188–191
deleting, 193
memory card, 178
sharing
email, 194
HDMI, 195
web browser, 194
slideshow, 193
transferring to/from PlayBook, 178–179
USB sharing on Mac, 182–183
USB sharing on Windows 7 PC, 179–181
viewing, 191
as wallpaper, 193
Wi-Fi sharing, 184–188
Photos application, editing, 193
Photos directory, 181
Pictures application, 191
albums, thumbnails, 192
deleting photos, 193
photos as wallpaper, 193
slideshows, 193
zooming, 193
PIM (personal information management),
102
Calendar, 102
appointments, 107–109
filtering services, 104–105
navigating, 104
service colors, 105
sources, 104
Tungle, 105
views, 102–103

Contacts
    creating, 110–112
    deleting, 110
    editing, 110
    viewing, 109–110
Memos, 115–116
Tasks, 112–114
Voice Notes, 116–118
pinch gesture, 45
Play/Pause button, 6
PlayBook
    buttons, 4
    as external drive, 148
    smartphone pairing, 79
    specifications, 3
playlists (Music app)
    adding, 149–150
    removing, 150
    RIM, 151
Podcasts app, 160
    downloading podcasts, 162–164
    subscribing to podcasts, 161–162
pop-ups, 70
portrait orientation, 49
    email, 94
    Web browsing, 63
    Word To Go, 123
ports
    HDMI, 8
    micro USB, 8
Power button, 6
Poynt, security settings, 243
preferences
    General, 271–272
    Storage and Sharing settings, 273–274
Presentation mode, indicator, 48
presentations
    rearranging, 141
    viewing, 140–141
pricing tier, 13
pulsing icons, 36

Q

QNX Neutrino Realtime Operating System
    (RTOS), 11

R

rear facing camera, 9
recharge battery, 288–289
recording video, 165–167
Redo, 126
Reminders for Tasks, 115
resolution
    battery life and, 267
    video capture, 166
restarting for troubleshooting, 288
retail box contents, 10
RIM (Research In Motion), 2
    playlists, 151
RTOS (Realtime Operating System), 11

S

Samsung Galaxy Tab, 16–17
screen display. *See* display
screens
    BlackBerry ID agreement, 27
    Connect to Wi-Fi, 21
    Date and Time, 26
    Home, 40
    Welcome screen, 20
screenshots
    storing captured, 193
    Volume button and, 8
scrolling, gestures, 42
SDK for Adobe Air, 12
search, email, 95
security, 70–72
    certificates, 244–246
    password
        changing, 251
        setting, 249–251
    permissions, applications, 240–244
    VPN files, 253–256
security wipe, 252–253, 292
selecting objects, gestures, 43
sharing
    File Sharing settings, 274
    Storage and Sharing setting, 273–274
Sharing toggle (Wi-Fi), 184
Sheet To Go, 131
    data linking, 138

number styles, 134
spreadsheets
    clearing cells, 136
    creating, 133–136
    editing, 136–137
    formulas, 137
    hiding cells, 136
    showing cells, 136
    text manipulation, 138
    transfer, 132
    viewing, 132
shortcuts, Bridge Browser, 83
Slacker Radio, 156–159
slideshow of photos, 193
Slideshow To Go, 139
    PlayBook presentations, 142
    presentations, viewing, 140–141
    rearranging slideshow, 141
smartphone
    PlayBook pairing, 79
    tethering, 263–267
software, updates, 29
Sounds Settings
    keyboard feedback, 270
    notifications, 270
    volume, 270
speakers, 4
specifications, 3
spreadsheets
    creating, 133–136
    editing, 136–137
    fonts, 133
    formulas, 137
    number styles, 134
    transferring to PlayBook, 132
    viewing, 132
stabilizing images at photo capture, 190
standby time-out, 268
startup, initial, 20–21
Status bar, 45
    gestures, 42
    icons, 48–49
    indicators, 48–49
    podcasts, 163
stereo speakers, 4
stopwatch, 215

storage, video, 166
Storage and Sharing setting, 184, 273–274
subscribing to podcasts, 161–162
swipe gesture, 41–43
Switch Devices, 286
switching between apps, 52–54
syncing
    Calendar, 105
    Media Sync, 283–284
    Tungle, 105

T

tabbed web browsing, 63–65
tablets
    comparisons, 13–14
        Apple iPad, 14
        Motorola Xoom, 14–15
        Samsung Galaxy Tab, 16–17
    sizes, 2
tabs
    categories, 35
    maximum open, 64
tapping, 43
Tasks, 112–114
    Reminders, 115
tethering smartphones, 263–267
Tetris, 205–208
text
    alignment, justified, 133
    fonts, 127
    formatting, 126–127
    spreadsheets, 138
thumbnail photos, 192
time. See also Date and Time setup
time-out
    backlight, 267–268
    standby, 268
timer, 215
Tip Calculator, 212–213
touch and hold, 44
touch methods. See gestures
transfers to PlayBook
    music, 147–148
        BlackBerry Desktop software,
        148–149

photos, 178–179
video, 165
troubleshooting
BlackBerry Bridge, 292–293
Bluetooth connection, 294–295
browser, 293–294
HDMI, 295
techniques
app updates, 290–291
battery recharge, 288–289
battery removal, 288
Home screen return, 289
PlayBook updates, 289–290
restarting, 288
security wipe, 292
Wi-Fi connection, 294
Tungle, 105
tutorials, 32–34
Twitter, Bridge, 90
.txt files, Word To Go, 124

U

underline text, 126
Undo, 126
unit converter on Calculator, 210–212
unstalling apps, 36–37
updates
apps, 290–291
software, 29
troubleshooting and, 289–290
USB for photo sharing
Mac, 182–183
Windows 7 PC, 179–181
USB port, 8
transferring music to PlayBook,
147–148

V

video, 164–165
Bridge Files, 81
capture resolution, 166
controls, 168
deleting, 166–167
HDMI viewing, 169
recording, 165–167

storage, 166
transferring to PlayBook, 165
video mode, 166
watching, 167–169
YouTube, 169–171
Video Chat
call notifications, 174–176
camera switch, 173
chat history, 174–175
Contacts, 172
ending call, 174
initiating session, 171–172
video conferencing, forward facing
camera, 5
Voice Notes
creating, 116–117
deleting, 118–119
file sizes, 118
playing, 118
recording levels, 118
volume
mute toggling, 7
Sounds Settings, 270
Volume button, 6
screenshots, 8
VPN (virtual private network), profile
creating, 253–254
deleting, 256

W

wallpaper
photos as, 193
setting, 34–35
Weather app, 198–200
weather application, menu, 51
web browser
Content options, 68–69
email, 97–98
Gmail view, 98
General settings, 67–68
Home screen, adding sites, 74
main menu, 67
menu, 50
permissions, 69–70
photo sharing, 194

privacy, 70–72
security, 70–72
web browsing, 60–61
bookmarks, 73–75
Bridge Browser, 82–84
cache clearing, 71
cookies, 70
downloads, 75
history, 65
Home screen
adding sites, 74
icon, 75
hyperlinks, 62
local storage, clearing, 72
navigation, 62–65
pop-ups, 70
portrait, 63
site access, 61
tabbed browsing, 63–65
Web Inspector, 71
websites on Home screen, 74
websockets, 71
Webworks SDK, 12
Welcome screen, 20
Wi-Fi
Bridge Browser, 82–83
connecting to, 21–22
listed networks, 23–24
manually, 24–25
connecting to PC, 147
connection, troubleshooting, 294
connection indicator, 49
hotspots, Bridge Browser, 60
photo sharing, 184–188

Sharing toggle, 184
tethering and, 263–267
transferring music to PlayBook, 147–148
WPS (Wi-Fi Protected Setup), 25–26
Windows 7
IP address, 187
USB photo sharing, 179–181
word count for documents, 127
Word To Go
documents
creating, 125–131
editing, 128–130
saving, 130–131
transferring, 124
viewing, 122–125
orientation, 123
.txt files, 124
zooming, 126
WPS (Wi-Fi Protected Setup), 25–26

X
Xoom, 14–15

Y
YouTube, viewing video, 169–171

Z
zoom
gestures, 43
photos, 193
Word To Go, 126